HISTORY AND GEOGRAPHY 1103
NATIONAL EXPANSION

CONTENTS

I. SHIP OF STATE 2

Federal Government 3

First Political Parties 8

II. REVOLUTION OF 1800 AND WAR OF 1812 18

The "Revolution" of 1800 18

The War of 1812 25

III. NATIONALISM AND SECTIONALISM 34

Nationalism and the Monroe Administration 36

Sectionalism and the Jackson Administration ... 41

Author: **Alpha Omega Staff**
Editor: Alan Christopherson M.S.
Illustrations: Alpha Omega Staff

Alpha Omega Publications®

804 N. 2nd Ave. E., Rock Rapids, IA 51246-1759
© MM by Alpha Omega Publications, Inc.   All rights reserved.
LIFEPAC is a registered trademark of Alpha Omega Publications, Inc.

HISTORY 1103
INTRODUCTION TO GOVERNMENT

A strong spirit of nationalism swept through the United States following the War of 1812. The war itself gave rise to increased feelings of self-confidence and unity. The peace that followed enabled the nation to concentrate on its own affairs. The bitterness that had marked political disputes eased with the break-up of the **Federalist Party**. Meanwhile, the nation expanded westward, new states entered the union, and the economy prospered. The period of history from 1815 to the early 1820s has often been called "The Era of Good Feelings" because of its relative peace, unity, and optimism about the nation's future.

In this unit we shall study the period immediately after the Constitutional Convention, the Revolution of 1800, the War of 1812, and, finally, the march of **democracy**.

OBJECTIVES

Read these objectives. The objectives tell you what you will be able to do when you have successfully completed this LIFEPAC®.

When you have finished this LIFEPAC, you should be able to:

1. List specific precedents set by President Washington in the absence of specific instructions in the Constitution.

2. Identify the four major components of Hamilton's plan to establish a sound financial program.

3. Compare the basic philosophies of Federalists and Democratic-Republicans.

4. Explain the factors leading to the rise of enduring political parties in the United States.

5. Discuss the source of the unexpected problems in the election of 1796 and the deadlocked election of 1800, indicating the outcome in each case and its implications.

6. Evaluate the extent of continuity and change in policies between the Democratic-Republican party that came to power in 1800 and the Federalist Party that preceded it.

7. Cite two examples of how President Jefferson lived up to his ideal of limited government to meet the needs of an agrarian society, and cite two instances in which he violated this idea.

8. Discuss the factors leading to the sale of the Louisiana Territory by France and its purchase by the United States.

9. Describe the impact of the Louisiana Purchase on American political and economic growth.

10. Discuss the War of 1812 and the political problems encountered by President Madison.

11. Describe the ways in which Chief Justice John Marshall's rulings established precedents for national supremacy over states' rights and defined the roles of the Court and Congress.

12. Explain the provisions of the Monroe Doctrine.

13. Identify the factors encouraging Western migration after 1820, and indicate the ways in which the rising importance of the West influenced the social, economic, and political trends of the rest of the country.

14. Discuss the role of slavery and economic depression in ending the "Era of Good Feelings" and precipitating a revival of sectional and political strife.

15. Cite factors that gave the common man new status during the Jacksonian era.

16. Describe the major characteristics of the two-party system during the Jacksonian era.

17. Trace the relationship between Jackson's view of the presidency and Thomas Jefferson's view and show how circumstances forced Jackson, like his predecessor, to support an activist federal government.

18. Describe the factions for and against the National Bank during the 1830s and the bank's role in the nation's history.

Survey the LIFEPAC. Ask yourself some questions about this study. Write your questions here.

_____

_____

_____

_____

_____

_____

_____

_____

_____

_____

_____

I. SHIP OF STATE

George Washington's **inauguration** was an occasion for nationwide rejoicing, but when the celebration had ended, the new nation had to face the serious business of building a government. Many details had to be added to the structure of the Constitution. The financial problems of the **republic** had to be dealt with, and the remaining differences of opinion about the function of government had to be reconciled.

Executive departments and a federal court system were created, and the jurisdiction of various courts was defined. The Bill of Rights, an especially important item for the **Antifederalists**, was passed by Congress and the states. These first ten amendments to the Constitution guaranteed certain individual liberties against the possible abuses of a powerful government.

The first secretary of the treasury, Alexander Hamilton, proposed a national bank and suggested that the federal government assume the debts incurred by the states during the Revolution. James Madison and many others objected to this part of Hamilton's plan, but a compromise involving the location of the nation's capital helped to resolve the problem.

Foreign affairs were even more difficult to settle. Troubles in Europe threatened American **neutrality**, and Europeans began seizing American merchant vessels on the high seas. President John Adams managed to avoid war despite the XYZ Affair and many protests from indignant Americans. Adam's foreign policy, the unpopular taxes enacted during his administration, and the controversy over the Alien and Sedition Acts combined to hasten the downfall of the Federalist Party. The election of 1800 ended in a victory for the **Democratic-Republicans** with Thomas Jefferson, the new president, announcing that the government ought to be open to all people of honesty, intelligence, and education.

SECTION OBJECTIVES

Review these objectives. When you have completed this section, you should be able to:

1. List specific precedents set by President Washington in the absence of specific instructions in the Constitution.

2. Identify the four major components of Hamilton's plan to establish a sound financial program.

3. Compare the basic philosophies of Federalists and Democratic-Republicans.

4. Explain the factors leading to the rise of enduring political parties in the United States.

5. Discuss the source of the unexpected problems in the election of 1796 and the deadlocked election of 1800, indicating the outcome in each case and its implications.

VOCABULARY

Study these words to enhance your learning success in this section.

Antifederalist – A member of a party opposed to the Federalists

cabinet – A group of advisors chosen by the head of a nation to help in government

caucus – A meeting of members of a political party to make plans, choose candidates or decide how to vote

democracy – A government run by the people who are under it. In a democracy, the people rule either directly through meetings that all may attend or indirectly through the election of representatives

electors – Members of the electoral college

electoral college – The group of people chosen by the voters to elect a president and vice president of the United States

excise tax – A tax on the manufacture, sell or use of certain articles

Federalist – A member or supporter of the Federalist Party in the United States

Federalist Party – A political party in the United States that favored the adoption of the Constitution and, later, the establishment of a strong central government; it existed from about 1791 to about 1816

impress – To force men to serve in the armed forces

inauguration – The act or ceremony of installing a president into office

neutrality – The attitude or policy of a nation that does not take part directly or indirectly in a war between other nations

republic – A nation or state in which the citizens elect representatives to manage the government, which is usually headed by a president rather than a monarch

Democratic-Republicans – Formed in 1792, favored a weak federal government and farmers

ratify – To confirm, approve

tariff – A list of duties or taxes that a government charges on imports or exports

Note: All vocabulary words in this LIFEPAC appear in **boldface** print the first time they are used. If you are unsure of the meaning when you are reading, study the definitions given.

FEDERAL GOVERNMENT

Although the **Federalists** had managed the first national election with considerable success, organizing the federal government presented new problems. The new administration also recognized the need to overcome any remaining fears of, and opposition to, a strong central government; and at the same time it had to win the respect of foreign nations.

The Constitution had gone into effect in 1789 when eleven states had **ratified** it. Within the next two years, North Carolina and Rhode Island had joined the Union. These thirteen states formed a country of roughly four million people. The Congress of the Confederation had asked the state to hold elections for presidential **electors**, representatives, and senators. The

electoral college met in February, 1789. Each elector cast two votes. The man receiving the largest number of votes was to become president, with the second choice becoming vice president. However, the results would not be known until the new Congress convened. Congress was scheduled to meet in March of 1789, but its members were so slow in assembling that the legislative body did not have a quorum until April.

First President. George Washington was elected president by unanimous vote and John Adams was elected vice president. However, Washington did not arrive in New York until late April. On April 30, 1789, he took the oath of office on the balcony of Federal Hall. The waiting crowds cheered. Washington then stepped back inside to read his **inaugural** address.

George Washington

The new president assumed his responsibilities with reluctance. He wrote: "My movement to the chair of government will be accompanied by feelings not unlike those of a culprit who is going to the place of his execution; so unwilling am I, in the evening of a life nearly consumed in public cares, to quit a peaceful abode for an ocean of difficulties."

The nation's strongest guarantee of success was its new president. Washington always considered carefully before making a decision, and once he had made a decision nothing could turn him from the course he thought right and proper. He knew that his actions would be a model for his successors, so he took great care from the beginning in establishing the government.

The Constitution made no mention of a presidential **cabinet**, but Washington established the custom of using the heads of various departments which Congress and the president established as his personal advisers. The departments that Washington established included the Department of Foreign Affairs (later renamed the Department of State), the Department of the Treasury, and the Department of War. A fourth executive position was established for the attorney general, who had the responsibility of handling the legal business of the government.

Thomas Jefferson was chosen as secretary of state because of his diplomatic experience abroad. Alexander Hamilton, a New York lawyer and a strong supporter of the Constitution, was made secretary of the treasury. Henry Knox, an army officer, became the secretary of war. The position of attorney general went to Edmund Randolph, who had helped to secure the ratification of the Constitution in Virginia.

Supreme Court. The Judiciary Act of 1789 provided for a Supreme Court made up of a Chief Justice and five associate justices. This act helped to strengthen the central government by permitting the Supreme Court to review state laws and state court decisions that involved the Constitution, treaties, and federal laws.

Bill of Rights. In 1789 Congress adopted the first ten amendments to the Constitution. These ten amendments are called the Bill of Rights because they guarantee the individual rights of American citizens. The primary author of these amendments was James Madison of Virginia. By the end of 1791 the amendments had been ratified by the states. Prompt action in adding the Bill of Rights to the Constitution did much to allay the fears of the **Antifederalists**. Taken together, the ten amendments are a statement of the American belief that the power of the government must be limited and its actions must be just. The Bill of Rights completed the American Revolution and ended the contest over the Constitution.

By September 1789, the legislators were ready to go home. However, one big problem still remained. The government was deeply in debt from the war and in need of new funding as well. Congress turned this problem over to Alexander Hamilton and asked him to prepare a report for Congress when it would reconvene in January of 1790.

Hamilton's financial program. Hamilton knew that the government could not run without money. He believed that credit was a matter of commitment that money lent would be repaid. To establish the credit of the government so that it could borrow money in the future, the treasury would have to pay its bad debts. The first part of Hamilton's program involved the payment of these debts. He proposed to issue government bonds bearing an interest of six percent and to offer them in exchange for the paper money and other debt certificates issued by the Continental Congress. In addition, he proposed that the federal government assume the debts incurred by the states in fighting the war. The Revolution was a common cause, Hamilton said; fairness required that the cost be borne by all.

Alexander Hamilton

The states that had already paid their debts objected on the grounds that they would, in essence, be paying their debts twice. Hamilton's proposals were not as simple as they seemed. The paper money and other certificates issued by the states during the Revolution had become practically worthless. Much of the money had fallen into the hands of a few speculators who had purchased it from the original holders for a fraction of the face value. To redeem it dollar for dollar meant a terrible burden for the government and an enormous windfall for the speculators.

Madison opposed Hamilton's plan, objecting to the windfall as being undeserved and expensive to the taxpayers. He also disliked the federal assumption of state debts. Madison received enough support in Congress to force Hamilton to compromise. In exchange for congressional approval to assume state debts, he agreed for the national capital to be moved to Philadelphia for ten years while a permanent capitol was being built on the banks of the Potomac River in Virginia. Hamilton got his financial system and the Virginians won the national capital.

The second part of Hamilton's program involved operating expenses for the government. He felt that as many expenses of the government as possible should be paid out of income taxes. His recommendation of various **excise taxes** (including a tax on the domestic manufacture of distilled liquor) as a means of supplementing the revenues obtained from the **tariff** were, for the most part, enacted by Congress. Hamilton accompanied troops into the field in 1794 to enforce the whiskey excise tax when the Whiskey Rebellion developed in western Pennsylvania.

The third part of Hamilton's program was a Bank of the United States. A national system of banking was the most important aspect of Hamilton's design. The system would be made up of a large central bank with branches in major cities. The bank would be chartered by Congress and would serve as an agent to the Treasury, holding funds on deposit and lending money to the government when necessary. The bank would have the power to issue money of its own—a sound, uniform currency backed by the bank's own reserves of gold and government bonds. The bank would help the government with the national debt. The new six percent bonds would hold their value because they could be exchanged for bank notes. Speculators, the main holders of government paper, would become the major stockholders in the bank through buying the shares with government bonds. The result would be a three-cornered pyramid: bank, government, and speculators. Out of this alliance would come firm government credit, a national currency, and political stability. In some respects, political stability was the most important.

Thomas Jefferson was one of many prominent men who opposed the bank because the power to make one was not mentioned in the Constitution. When the bill for the bank reached President Washington, he ask Jefferson and Hamilton to write papers on whether or not the bank was constitutional. After Washington studied the two papers, he decided that the idea of a national bank was sound, and he accepted Hamilton's viewpoint that the president had the implied power from the Constitution to charter such an institution. In February 1791, Washington signed the controversial bank bill into law. The furor over the national bank had sharpened the differences between those who wanted to strengthen the central government and those who wanted to limit it; between those who favored the economic interests of merchants and manufacturers and those who sided with the planters

and farmers; and between those who agreed with Hamilton and those who agreed with Madison and Jefferson.

The fourth part of Hamilton's financial program dealt with metal currency. Since colonial days, America had suffered a shortage of coins. Much confusion had resulted from the use of a variety of foreign coins. On Hamilton's recommendation, Congress passed the Mint Act of 1792, which provided for the minting of gold, silver, and copper coins based on the decimal system.

Match these items.

1.1	_____ democracy	a.	the act or ceremony of installing a president into office
1.2	_____ cabinet	b.	the attitude or policy of a nation that does not take part directly or indirectly
1.3	_____ inauguration	c.	to confirm, approve
1.4	_____ neutrality	d.	a government run by the people who are under it
1.5	_____ ratify	e.	a group of advisors chosen by the head of a nation to help in government
1.6	_____ tariff	f.	a list of duties or taxes that a government charges on imports or exports

Match the following.

1.7	_____ Antifederalist	a.	the group of people chosen by the voters to elect a president and vice president
1.8	_____ Federalist Party	b.	a tax on the manufacture, sell or use of certain articles
1.9	_____ electoral college	c.	a member of a party opposed to the Federalists
1.10	_____ excise tax	d.	a member or supporter of the Federalist Party in the United States
1.11	_____ Democratic-Republicans	e.	members of the electoral college
1.12	_____ Federalist	f.	a nation or state in which the citizens elect representatives
1.13	_____ republic	g.	a political party in the United States that favored the adoption of the Constitution
1.14	_____ electors	h.	party that wanted a weak federal government

Write the letter of the correct answer(s) on the blank.

1.15 Washington's election to the presidency was important because _____
   a. he considered every problem thoughtfully and followed through.
   b. he had the respect of some of the people.
   c. he chose bad advisors.

1.16   Washington's main objective as president of the United States was to _____
        a. maintain his power and get reelected.
        b. keep peace between the northern and southern states.
        c. establish respect for the office of the presidency.
        d. set up a court similar to that of European monarchs.

1.17   Hamilton proposed paying the entire national debt at its face value in order to _____
        a. win the support of the congressmen who had speculated in government certificates.
        b. reimburse only the original holders of certificates who still possessed them.
        c. restore the nation's economic credit so that the government could raise money in the future.
        d. keep to a minimum the amount of money paid by the government.

1.18   The executive departments established were: _____ , _____ , _____ , _____ .
        a. the State Department
        b. the Labor Department
        c. the Treasury Department
        d. the Welfare Department
        e. the War Department
        f. the Education Department
        g. the Attorney General's office

1.19   The Judiciary Act of 1789 _____
        a. did not provide a way to finance the courts.
        b. provided for a chief justice and five associate justices.
        c. kept the court from touching any matter that involved the Constitution.

1.20   Hamilton justified the establishment of a national bank: _____ , _____ , _____ .
        a. by having it hold funds
        b. by lending money
        c. by closing on mortgages
        d. by developing currency

True/False.

1.21   _____   The Constitution made no mention of a presidential cabinet.

Fill in the blank.

1.22   _____ established the custom of using the heads
        of various departments for his personal advisers.

1.23   The national bank was opposed by many because it was not mentioned in the
        _____ .

FIRST POLITICAL PARTIES

The split between Hamilton, who believed in government by the wealthy and powerful, and Jefferson and Madison, who had faith in the common people, was the first crack in the ranks of those who had drafted the Constitution. The conflict was more than a clash of individual personalities. Hamilton's support was chiefly northern and mercantile. To promote American manufacturing and make the United States independent of European goods, Hamilton suggested raising tariffs to protect American industry from foreign competition. Jefferson and Madison, both from the rural South, opposed Hamilton's plan, fearing that it would destroy foreign trade and foreign markets for American farm exports. Out of such regional and economic differences, the first political parties were formed.

In the autumn of 1791, Jefferson and Madison established a newspaper, *The National Gazette*, to acquaint the public with their views. By the end of the year, the opposition group had become known as the Democratic-Republicans or Republicans for short. The choice of that name was a shrewd one because it suggested that Jefferson and Madison were the true defenders of the republic and that their Hamiltonian opponents were monarchists in disguise. The Hamiltonians chose to call themselves the Federalist Party and hinted broadly that their opponents were Antifederalists. Although many Republicans felt that Washington too often sided with Hamilton, Jefferson and Madison continued to respect the president. Washington was reelected in 1792 by the unanimous vote of the electoral college. John Adams remained vice president.

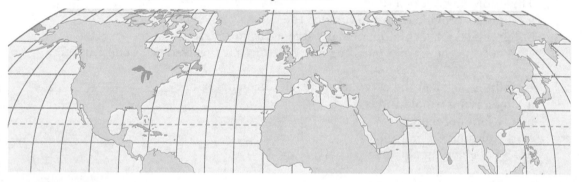

Foreign affairs. Problems of foreign affairs facing the new nation were the French Revolution, British seizure of American ships, a treaty with England, and a treaty with Spain.

In 1789 the French Revolution began. Since it was a revolt of the people against an absolute monarchy, Americans greeted the uprising enthusiastically. "In no part of the globe," wrote an American lawyer, "was this revolution hailed with more joy than in America." At first, Americans were sympathetic with the French Revolution, but as more and more emphasis was placed on **democracy** and the rights of the common man, the Federalists became alarmed. When the king was beheaded, even the most liberal Federalists lost sympathy. The Republicans disapproved of the violence, but they hoped that it would soon give way to an orderly democratic government.

Worried and uncertain about how to react to France, President Washington asked the advice of Hamilton, Jefferson, and the rest of his cabinet. It was agreed that, despite the friendship between the United States and France, their country should stay out of the European war. Although Jefferson believed that the United States should still honor its treaty with France, he realized that the United States was too weak to wage war. President Washington signed an official paper declaring that the United States would be "friendly and impartial" to both sides in the war. In other words, the United States would remain neutral.

In the spring of 1793, France sent a special envoy to America, Edmond Charles Genet. Genet wanted to enlist Americans to serve on French warships, and he hoped to gain permission to use American ports as French naval bases. When the administration insisted on strict neutrality, Genet took his case to the newspapers, hoping to play upon the pro-French feelings of American people. Instead, his bullying tone rallied supporters to the president, injured the French cause, and embarrassed Republicans. Jefferson breathed a sigh of relief when the French government recalled its inept ambassador.

Although the United States declared its neutrality in the European war, that neutrality was not easy to maintain. Countries at war object if they believe that any act of a neutral nation will harm them or will help their enemies. When the United States declared that as a neutral nation it had the right to trade with the warring nations, trouble began.

Seizure of American ships. The chief threat to America's neutrality came from Great Britain, owner of the world's most powerful navy. She did not intend to permit the United States to aid the French by shipping them the goods they needed. Britain, therefore, set out to stop such trade. Time and again, British warships would stop American schooners, search them, and seize the cargo if they determined that the schooner was breaking the British rules of the sea. The British officer might then examine the crew, declare that some of them were British sailors, and take them to his ship to **impress** them into the Royal Navy. Whether the sailors were American citizens mattered little; to the British, "born an Englishman" meant "always an Englishman."

A second grievance was that the British still occupied forts along the northwestern boundary of the United States. The British held the forts and stationed soldiers there because Americans had not paid certain debts and because England wanted to profit from the fur trade on American soil.

Treaty with England. In spite of these difficulties with the British, President Washington worked to maintain peace. In 1794 he sent John Jay, the Chief Justice of the Supreme Court, to Europe to seek an agreement with the British government. Washington hoped that such an agreement would put an end to the trouble between the two countries. Jay did obtain an agreement. Among other things, Jay's Treaty stated that the British should turn over the forts along the Great Lakes to the United States. However, the British did not promise to stop searching American ships and impressing American sailors.

MOUNT VERNON

For this reason, many Americans disliked Jay's Treaty. The treaty was approved in 1795, however, and Washington's judgment proved correct—the danger of war between the two countries was removed for the time being. The treaty was important for two other reasons: (1) It marked this country's first use of negotiation as a means of settling an international dispute, and (2) it prepared the way for settlement of the long dispute with Spain.

Treaty with Spain. The Spanish government was afraid that the United States, with her British troubles settled, might threaten the safety of Spanish Florida or Louisiana. Late in 1795, therefore, Thomas Pinckney was sent to conclude a treaty with Spain. Pinckney's Treaty fixed the boundary between the United States and West Florida at the thirty-first parallel, and it guaranteed navigation rights on the Mississippi to American citizens. Spain also granted the use of New Orleans as a "port of deposit," where American goods could be transferred from riverboats to ocean-going vessels without payment of regular duties. Westerners were pleased with this treaty, but they still hoped that New Orleans would eventually come under American control.

Farewell address of Washington. As Washington's second term drew to a close, he looked forward to retirement at Mount Vernon. Bitter personal attacks by political opponents and the constant quarrels between the Federalists and the Republicans had saddened him. In 1796 his "Farewell Address" warning American citizens of the evils of sectional jealousy and "the baneful effects of the spirit of party" was published in the newspapers. Washington emphasized the need for continued neutrality and urged the country "to steer clear of permanent alliances with any portion of the foreign world." His "Farewell Address" has become one of this country's important public documents.

FEDERALIST PRESIDENT

As the election of 1796 drew near, the rivalry between the Federalists and the Republicans became more intense. The Federalists in Congress held a private conference, or **caucus**, and urged the election of John Adams for the presidency and Thomas Pinckney for the vice presidency. A Republican caucus recommended Jefferson (pictured) for president and Aaron Burr, a Republican leader in New York, for vice president.

Since Hamilton was not on good terms with Adams, he attempted to influence the electoral vote so that Pinckney would win. To that end, he appealed to southern Federalist electors to vote only for Pinckney, who came from South Carolina; but Adams' New England supporters, having learned of this trick, withheld electoral votes from Pinckney. The result was that

Thomas Jefferson

Adams, a Federalist, was elected president by seventy-one electoral votes and Jefferson, a Republican, became vice president with sixty-eight votes. Pinckney came in third with fifty-nine.

John Adams was a man of ability and absolute honesty, never swerving from what he believed to be right; however, he was not a popular president. His main contribution was keeping the United States at peace during a time when the country could ill afford war.

Soon after Jay's Treaty with Great Britain had been signed, serious trouble began between the United States and France. Jay's Treaty itself was partly to blame. The French thought that the treaty showed Americans more friendly to Britain than to France.

National Archives

John Adams

10

The French decided that American ships should not be allowed to carry goods that might reach their enemies. Following the example set by Britain, the French began to capture American ships.

The XYZ Affair. War with Great Britain had been avoided during Washington's administration by sending John Jay to arrange a treaty. John Adams followed Washington's example, attempting to avoid war with France by sending three men to arrange a treaty. At the beginning of their talks, the French representatives demanded the payment of a large amount of money before they would even talk about a treaty. The Americans proudly refused to pay what they felt was a bribe and wrote to the president to tell him what had happened. In their letters, however, they did not use the real names of the three French representatives, referring to them instead as X, Y, and Z. For this reason the event is known as the XYZ Affair.

An undeclared war with France. Many people in the United States were angered by the XYZ Affair. "Millions for defense," they cried, "but not one cent for tribute!" The few naval vessels which the government had built attacked French vessels, and armed American ships of all kinds captured French ships whenever they could. Despite the fighting, however, the United States and France were not officially at war, since Congress had never declared that a state of war existed. Although the feeling against France was at its height, President Adams learned that the French government wanted to end the conflict. In 1800 an agreement was signed, ending the alliance made during the Revolution and clearing the way for ships of both nations to sail in peace.

The Alien and Sedition Acts. The Republican Party was gaining new members rapidly. Many of the immigrants who came to this country in the 1790s joined the Republican Party. Alarmed by this development, the Federalists decided to use the quarrel with France as an excuse for striking out at the Republicans. Claiming a national emergency, they forced four controversial measures through Congress in 1798.

The first of these measures, the Naturalization Act, required a foreigner to live in the United States for fourteen years, rather than for five years, before he could become a citizen and vote. The Alien Act permitted the president to deport aliens whom he judged "dangerous to the peace and safety of the United States." A related act called the Alien Enemies Act permitted the president to imprison or deport dangerous aliens in time of war. The fourth measure, the Sedition Act, authorized fines up to $5,000 and imprisonment for as long as five years for anyone who tried to hinder the operation of the government.

The Sedition Act was aimed specifically at Republican newspapers. It prescribed punishment for anyone who wrote or published "false, scandalous and malicious" statements against the government, Congress or the president, as well as statements that tended to "stir up sedition." Many Republican newspaper editors were fined and jailed.

The Alien and Sedition Acts were a costly mistake. Both Republicans and Federalists criticized them. The Republicans denounced the laws as violations of the First Amendment, which guarantees freedom of speech and of the press. The Kentucky legislature drew up and adopted a set of resolutions which held that the federal government had been formed by a compact among the states through which certain powers were given by the states to the central government. Since the states had not specifically granted Congress any power to pass the Alien and Sedition Acts, those acts were illegal. In such a situation, according to the Kentucky resolution, the only recourse the states had was to declare the acts of Congress "unauthoritative, void, and of no force" within their boundaries.

National Archives

James Madison

The Virginia legislature approved a similar set of resolutions drafted by James Madison. Both sets of resolutions raised a fundamental question—whether a state had the right to declare an act of Congress unlawful. The most immediate effect of the Kentucky and Virginia resolutions, however, was to provide ammunition for the Republicans in the election of 1800.

By the end of the 1790s, many of the country's small farmers, skilled workers, and tradesmen had become members of the Republican Party. Led by Madison and Jefferson, the Republicans attacked the whole Federalist program: Hamilton's financial policy, loose interpretation of the Constitution, the growing centralization of government, increased taxes, failure to reduce the debt, and the money spent on the army and navy.

The election of 1800. The Federalist candidates lost the election of 1800. However, the two Republican candidates, Thomas Jefferson and Aaron Burr, each had seventy-three electoral votes. This tie meant that the House of Representatives had to choose between Jefferson and Burr for the presidency. The Federalists could throw the election either way. Though Hamilton intensely disliked Jefferson, he knew that Burr was a man without principles. With Hamilton's support, Jefferson was elected on the thirty-sixth ballot. The inefficiency of the system became evident, and in 1804 the Twelfth Amendment was adopted, allowing the electors to cast separate ballots for president and vice president.

Efforts to preserve Federalist principles. During the closing days of Adams' administration, Congress passed a Judiciary Act establishing a number of new positions for judges. Adams hoped that these judges would keep Federalist views alive. A greater influence in preserving the Federalist principles, however, was the appointment several weeks earlier of John Marshall as Chief Justice of the Supreme Court.

Fill in the blank.

1.24   A _____ is a meeting of the members of a political party.

1.25   Leaders of the two political parties were Hamilton of the _____

Party and Madison and Jefferson of the _____ Party.

1.26   To _____ is to force men to serve in the armed forces.

1.27   The United States did not take either side in the French Revolution but adopted a position

of strict _____ .

1.28   Jay's Treaty with England was unpopular in the United States because the British did not

promise to stop interfering with American _____ .

1.29   Pinckney's Treaty with Spain finally solved the problem of the boundary between the U.S.

and _____ .

1.30   The emphasis of Washington's "Farewell Address" was to not make any permanent

_____ .

1.31   The French reacted to Jay's Treaty with England by beginning to
        _____ American ships.

1.32   In response to President Adams' efforts to reach an understanding, the French requested
        _____ before talks would begin.

1.33   Which states declared the Alien and Sedition Acts void and of no force within their boundaries?
        _____ and _____

1.34   Because of the Alien and Sedition Acts and because of its unpopular policies, the
        _____ Party lost its popular support and the election of 1800.

1.35   A separate vote for president and vice president was required by the _____
        Amendment to the Constitution.

True/False.

1.36   _____   Those who opposed Hamilton's financial policies were northern merchants who
                believed in government by the wealthy and powerful.

1.37   _____   Opposition to Hamilton's policies led to the organization of the Republican Party and
                the Federalist Party.

1.38   _____   The XYZ Affair got its name because the American envoys refused to name the three
                English officials who demanded a large amount of money before they would even dis-
                cuss a treaty.

1.39   _____   The terms of the settlement reached with France in 1800 cleared the way for peaceful
                sailing.

Match these items.

1.40   _____   Naturalization Act   a. authorized fines up to $5,000 and imprisonment for
                                               hindering government

1.41   _____   Alien and Sedition Acts   b. an effort to preserve Federalist principles

1.42   _____   Alien Act   c. a foreigner had to live in the United States fourteen years
                                               to become a citizen

1.43   _____   Alien Enemies Act   d. series of laws which took advantage of war hysteria to
                                               control the Republicans

1.44   _____   Judiciary Act   e. permitted the president to imprison or deport dangerous
                                               aliens in time of war

1.45   _____   Sedition Act   f. permitted the president to deport aliens whom he
                                               judged "dangerous"

Choose the best answer.

1.46   The Kentucky and Virginia resolutions, made in opposition to the Alien and Sedition Acts: _____
        a. once and for all determined that the national government was sovereign in the United States.
        b. claimed that the states could nullify any actions by the federal government that they
            judged unconstitutional.
        c. forced the repeal of the acts.
        d. brought a new prestige to the federal court system.

 **Adult Check**   _____
                                    Initial   Date

 Review the material in this section in preparation for the Self Test. The Self Test will check
your mastery of this particular section. The items missed on this Self Test will indicate specific
areas where restudy is needed for mastery.

SELF TEST 1

True/False (each answer, 2 points).

1.01 _____ Hamilton's economic measures were prompted by his determination to strengthen the national government.

1.02 _____ Thomas Pickney's treaty with Spain won for the United States free navigation of the Mississippi and permission for American traders to deposit goods for shipment at the mouth of the river.

1.03 _____ Alexander Hamilton, Edmund Randolph, Henry Knox, and James Madison were the men chosen by President Washington to serve in the first cabinet.

1.04 _____ The first political parties were formed around regional and economic differences.

1.05 _____ The XYZ Affair involved relations between the United States and England.

1.06 _____ The Alien and Sedition Acts were a costly mistake for the Federalists because they were contrary to the ideas found in the Bill of Rights.

1.07 _____ The United States could not reach acceptable terms of settlement with France regarding peaceful shipping.

Choose one answer (each answer, 2 points).

1.08 Washington's main objective as president of the United States was to _____ .
   a. maintain his power and get reelected
   b. keep peace between the northern and southern states
   c. establish respect for the office of the presidency
   d. set up a court similar to that of European monarchs

1.09 Hamilton proposed paying the entire national debt at its face value in order to _____ .
   a. win the support of the congressmen who had speculated in government certificates
   b. reimburse only the original holders of certificates who still possessed them
   c. restore the nation's economic credit so that the government could raise money in the future
   d. keep to a minimum the amount of money paid by the government

1.010 Many Americans opposed Hamilton's proposal to have the national government assume debts owed by the states because _____ .
   a. many people did not want speculators to gain profits from the scheme
   b. the Republicans feared that the national government would get too powerful
   c. states that had already paid a large proportion of their debt would have to help pay the debts of other states
   d. all of the above

1.011 Washington's proclamation of neutrality of 1793 was _____ .
   a. issued to prevent England from marching troops through American territory in order to attack Spaniards in Louisiana
   b. prompted by Jefferson's horror at the destructive aspects of the French Revolution
   c. supported by Washington's French ally, citizen Genet
   d. made because the United States was too weak to wage war

15

1.012　　　The United States was brought to the brink of war with England in 1794 because of _____ .
　　　　a.　British seizure of American ships and impressment of American seamen
　　　　b.　Hamilton's war-mongering policies
　　　　c.　Citizen Genet's subversive activities on behalf of the French government
　　　　d.　Congress' anger at the British retention of total control of the Mississippi River

1.013　　　The following item was a factor in ending the alliance between France and the United States _____ .
　　　　a.　fighting between French and American ships
　　　　b.　French interception and impounding of American vessels bound for England
　　　　c.　the XYZ Affair wherein a high monetary price was placed as a condition for a treaty with France
　　　　d.　all of the above

1.014　　　The Alien and Sedition Acts were designed to _____
　　　　a.　keep the number of foreign immigrants to the United States at a minimum.
　　　　b.　give a formal recognition to the party system within the American government.
　　　　c.　restrain Republican opposition to the Federalist administration.
　　　　d.　all of the above.

1.015　　　The Kentucky and Virginia resolutions, made in opposition to the Alien and Sedition Acts, _____
　　　　a.　once and for all determined that the national government was sovereign in the United States.
　　　　b.　claimed that the states could nullify any actions by the federal government that they judged unconstitutional.
　　　　c.　forced the repeal of the acts.
　　　　d.　brought a new prestige to the federal court system.

1.016　　　The Twelfth Amendment to the Constitution, adopted in 1804, _____
　　　　a.　required the electoral college to vote separately for president and vice president.
　　　　b.　created a new federal judiciary system with John Marshall as Chief Justice of the United States.
　　　　c.　institutionalized the two-party system in American politics.
　　　　d.　established the sovereignty of the national government over the state governments.

Match the following (each answer, 2 points).

1.017　　_____　Jefferson　　　　　　a.　drafter of the Bill of Rights

1.018　　_____　Hamilton　　　　　　b.　first secretary of state

1.019　　_____　Madison　　　　　　c.　first secretary of the treasury

1.020　　_____　Jay　　　　　　　　d.　French representative sent to United States to seek American support against Britain

1.021　　_____　Pinckney　　　　　　e.　second president of the United States

1.022　　_____　Adams　　　　　　　f.　attorney general under Washington

1.023　　_____　Genet　　　　　　　g.　minister to Britain who negotiated a treaty in 1795

1.024　　_____　Randolph　　　　　　h.　envoy to Spain who negotiated the 1796 treaty that guaranteed free navigation

Match the Acts with their descriptions (each answer, 2 points).

1.025 _____ Alien Enemies Act
          a. permitted the president to imprison or deport danger-ous aliens in time of war

1.026 _____ Judiciary Act
          b. foreigners had to live in U.S. 14 years before becoming citizens

1.027 _____ Sedition Act
          c. an effort to preserve Federalist principles

1.028 _____ Naturalization Act
          d. were considered a costly mistake for the Federalists

1.029 _____ Alien and Sedition Acts
          e. permitted the president to deport aliens whom he judged "dangerous"

1.030 _____ Alien Act
          f. authorized fines up to $5,000 for those hindering government operation

Fill in the blanks (each answer, 3 points).

1.031 The _____ reacted to Jay's Treaty with England by beginning to capture American _____ .

1.032 In response to President Adams' efforts to reach an understanding regarding the capture of American ships, the French requested _____ before talks would begin.

1.033 Which states declared the Alien and Sedition Acts void and of no force within their boundaries? _____ and _____

1.034 Because of the Alien and Sedition Acts and because of its unpopular policies, the _____ Party lost its popular support and the election of 1800.

62/78

II. REVOLUTION OF 1800 AND WAR OF 1812

In his later years, Jefferson was fond of saying that "the Revolution of 1800 was as real a revolution in the principles of our government as that of 1776 was in its form." Jefferson and his secretary of the treasury trimmed the edges of Hamilton's financial system; however, they left its keystone, the national bank, undisturbed. The Republicans could do little about the Federalist control of the judiciary. They had to accept Marshall's decisions, strengthening the hand of the central government. In foreign affairs, Jefferson kept his inaugural promise of no "entangling alliances." He showed favoritism to neither France nor Britain and managed to avoid war with both countries.

During his presidency, Jefferson's actions sometimes conflicted with the principles he had expounded in the 1790s. He increased expenditures for the navy, engaged in war with the Barbary pirates, and added territory to the Union, even though the Constitution did not specifically authorize him to do so. Jefferson was wise enough to see that the country would gain by these measures. "What is practicable must often control what is pure theory," he said. Historians agree that Jefferson's decision to sign the Louisiana Treaty, in spite of his doubts about its constitutionality, was an act of statesmanship.

President Jefferson's hopes for "peaceful coercion" through the Embargo Act were not fulfilled. He found no formula for protecting American rights on the seas, but he did leave to his successor a country that was still neutral in the Napoleonic Wars.

SECTION OBJECTIVES

Review these objectives. When you have completed this section, you should be able to:

6. Evaluate the extent of continuity and change in policies between the Republican Party that came to power in 1800 and the Federalist Party that preceded it.

7. Cite two examples of how President Jefferson lived up to his ideal of limited government to meet the needs of an agrarian society and cite two instances in which he violated this ideal.

8. Discuss the factors leading to the sale of the Louisiana Territory by France and its purchase by the United States.

9. Describe the impact of the Louisiana Purchase on American political and economic growth.

10. Discuss the War of 1812 and the political problems encountered by President Madison.

VOCABULARY

Study these words to enhance your learning success in this section.

blockade – Control of who or what goes into or out of a place, especially by police or by an army or by a navy

boycott – To refuse to buy or use (a product or service); to join together against and having nothing to do with (a person, business, nation, employer or any other person or thing) in order to coerce or punish

embargo – An order of a government forbidding merchant ships to enter or leave its ports

suffrage – The right to vote

THE "REVOLUTION" OF 1800

To the end of his days, Jefferson referred to his election to the presidency as "the Revolution of 1800" because Jefferson believed that the future of the Republic was at stake in his struggle with John Adams.

One of his first acts as president was to release those who were still in jail as a result of the Sedition Act. Jefferson believed that the strength of a government depended upon its popularity and not upon its use of force.

Inauguration Day, March 4, 1801, dawned chilly and rainy upon the half-built Capitol on the banks of the Potomac. John Adams, unable to bear his foe's triumph, slipped out of town at four o'clock in the morning. Jefferson, dressed in a plain dark suit and without badge or sword, walked down from his boardinghouse to the Capitol where he was given the oath of office.

Except for a salute by the Maryland militia, not a shot had been fired, not a soldier had been seen. "I have this morning witnessed one of the most interesting scenes," wrote Margaret Bayard Smith, wife of a Republican newspaper editor. "The changes of administration, which in every government and in every age have most generally been epochs of confusion, villainy, and bloodshed, in this our happy country take place without any disorder." The orderly transfer of power was a measure of the young republic's political maturity.

Jefferson's term of office was not quite the "revolution" that he later remembered. No widespread dismissal of Federalist officeholders occurred, nor were the Federalist programs totally removed. Jefferson kept and used the Bank of the United States; the Alien and Sedition laws had already expired. The atmosphere had changed. John Adams had considered the Federalist Party to be the party of the "rich and well-born," and he had stocked the government offices with people of family and fortune. Jefferson announced that the government ought to be open to all people of honesty, intelligence, and education.

Wise and frugal government. Jefferson was particularly concerned that government not be a burden. Together with his secretary of the treasury, Albert Gallatin, Jefferson eliminated all internal excise taxes, instead securing income for the government from customs duties and the sale of western lands. To save money, Jefferson and Gallatin reduced the army to three thousand soldiers and sold most of the navy's vessels. Jefferson's aim, stated in his inaugural address, was "a wise and frugal government" that would leave citizens alone "to regulate their own pursuits of industry and profit."

Albert Gallatin

Open, responsive, and concerned government was the essence of the "Revolution of 1800." Jefferson's administration was also, as he had predicted, the beginning of popular government in the United States. Jefferson had swamped the Federalist opposition in the presidential election of 1804, and his party had achieved control of Congress. However, America was not yet a democracy. Most states still had property requirements for voting and office holding, and white males over twenty-one were still the only people allowed to vote. Inspired by Jefferson's concern for the common citizen, several states began modifying their property requirements for **suffrage**.

Marbury v. Madison. During Jefferson's term of office the power of the Supreme Court was increased. William Marbury, one of the judges appointed by Adams before he left office, had not been granted his commission of office prior to the change of administration. Marbury asked the Supreme Court to compel Secretary of State James Madison to grant him his commission. Chief Justice John Marshall recognized that if he and the justices approved Marbury's request, Madison might not follow the Court's orders, thus weakening the people's respect for the judiciary. If the justices rejected Marbury's request, however, the Republicans would have an apparent victory. Marshall managed to avoid both political pitfalls. In his decision, he stated that Marbury deserved the commission but that the Court was powerless to make the secretary of state deliver it because of a conflict between the Constitution and the Judiciary Act of 1789.

Marshall's decision in *Marbury v. Madison* was a blow to the Republicans, but it strengthened the federal judiciary by establishing the principle that the Supreme Court could declare acts of Congress unconstitutional. This ruling was the first of many important decisions made by John Marshall during his thirty-five years as Chief Justice.

Trouble in Europe. While France and England were at war in Europe, Spain had changed sides, going back with its former ally, France. Fearing that Britain might seize Louisiana, Spain's territory west of the Mississippi River, Spain secretly gave Louisiana to France for protection. Spain expected to have the territory returned to her at the end of the war.

Knowing that the United States would disapprove of the bargain, the two countries kept it secret, and Spain continued to govern the territory. Jefferson learned of the deal, however, and exploded in anger. He did not want a strong military power like France on his nation's western border, but as long as Spanish officials remained in New Orleans he could do little about it.

In 1802 Napoleon took advantage of a truce in the European war by sending an army to America. The French army first recaptured the island of Santo Domingo, settled by black slaves who had revolted and declared their independence. The French then occupied Louisiana. Anticipating the French arrival, Spanish authorities closed the port of New Orleans to American traffic. The American reaction was violent. Cut off from its markets and threatened with economic strangulation, the West was understandably angry.

To ease the situation, Jefferson sent a special envoy to Paris. His choice was James Monroe, his friend from Virginia. Jefferson told Monroe either to buy New Orleans or to persuade Napoleon to open the port.

James Monroe

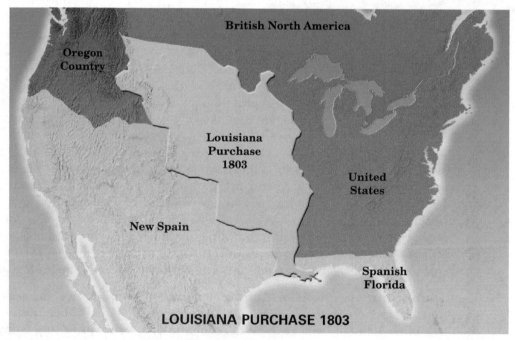

LOUISIANA PURCHASE 1803

The Louisiana Purchase. By the time Monroe arrived in Paris, the situation had changed dramatically. Napoleon's army had not been victorious in Santo Domingo, and many of his troops had been killed by yellow fever. He could no longer defend Louisiana. Expecting a renewal of the war with Britain, he was also in need of money. Since Louisiana seemed useless, he decided to sell it.

Napoleon summoned Robert Livingston, America's regular minister in Paris, and offered to sell not only New Orleans but the whole inland empire drained by the

Mississippi and Missouri rivers. At first, Livingston balked at Napoleon's price—$15 million, which included war debts owed to France—but he ultimately agreed. The two were coming to terms when Monroe arrived. Monroe cooperated and the treaty of purchase was signed in May of 1803.

Although Monroe and Livingston had not followed their instructions—had bought an empire rather than a city and had paid fifty percent more than they had been authorized to spend—Jefferson was delighted with their purchase. "An empire for liberty," he called it; it would provide room and freedom for generations to come.

Jefferson worried about whether he had the power to make the purchase. The Constitution does not specifically authorize the president either to buy or to conquer foreign territory. His cabinet, however, persuaded him to submit the treaty to the Senate.

In Congress, New England Federalists bitterly opposed the purchase, knowing that the new territory would further weaken their influence in the Union. They argued that the Constitution did not give the federal government the power to buy territory and that new territory could be added only with the consent of the original thirteen states. Jefferson's use of executive power and the Federalists' opposition to it was a curious reversal of roles, an indication of how ideas can change when people's situations and interests change. The Senate, however, approved the treaty, and the House of Representatives quickly appropriated the money required to fulfill the treaty's terms.

Reelection of Jefferson. Meanwhile, in the election of 1804, the Republican prospects for victory had been heightened by several factors: the country was prosperous, taxes had been cut, and the national debt had been reduced in spite of the Louisiana Purchase.

Although the changes had been less drastic than the Federalists had predicted, they were very real. The idea that the average citizen should have a share in the government was gaining acceptance, and the nation was becoming more democratic.

One problem facing Jefferson during both his terms in the White House was the protection of American neutral rights on the seas. Pirates in the Mediterranean continued to plague American shipping. Washington and Adams, like the rulers of European countries, had paid tribute to the Barbary pirates. Jefferson disliked paying tribute, so he decided to send a small American squadron to the Mediterranean in 1801. For four years the American navy blockaded and bombarded Tripoli, finally forcing it to sign a favorable treaty in 1805. Soon afterward, agreements were reached with other North African countries. The raids of the Barbary pirates ended in 1816 with the defeat of Algeria.

Napoleon

Protection of American rights. When Britain and France renewed warfare in 1803, Napoleon had managed to gain control of a large part of Europe. England remained mistress of the sea. Great Britain issued orders in council declaring that if neutral ships went into European ports controlled by Napoleon, they would no longer be considered neutral by the British.

Napoleon, on the other hand, issued a number of decrees with the intention of stopping British exports from reaching European ports. Since both countries wanted to buy American foodstuffs, both encouraged American shippers to trade exclusively with them. The Americans were caught in the bewildering crossfire of British orders and French decrees. Once again, American neutral rights were in danger.

In spite of the threats, American trade prospered. High prices for merchandise brought such fantastic profits that a merchant made money even if only a third of his ships succeeded in running the **blockade** and landing their cargo.

Impressment of seamen. Of greater concern to many Americans was the continued practice by the British of impressing American seamen. The British navy was always in need of seamen. One reason for this need was that hundreds of deserters from the British navy had found work on United States ships where working conditions and pay were better. The British claimed the right to stop neutral ships on the high seas, remove sailors of British birth, and impress or force them back into British naval service. The United States objected strongly to this practice because many native-born Americans were impressed "by mistake."

The matter was brought to a head by the "*Chesapeake* Affair." The *Chesapeake* was an American ship boarded by the British under false pretenses. When the American officer refused to allow a search for deserters, the British officer returned to his ship and fired on the *Chesapeake*, killing three sailors. The British commander then reboarded the *Chesapeake* and took four men he said were deserters—three of them were American citizens. Following the "*Chesapeake* Affair" many Americans demanded war. Congress appropriated funds to increase the size of the navy. Even while building the navy, Congress gave the president a chance to try "peaceable means of repressing injustice."

Jefferson decided to try an **embargo** on trade to exert pressure on Great Britain. The idea was good, but a bumper crop in England made the embargo only slightly felt there. In America, however, the **boycott** hurt business. Warehouses were bursting with products that could not be shipped, grass began to grow on the wharves, and shipbuilding came to a halt. In general, the American economy was badly hurt by the embargo. Not wanting his successor James Madison to be saddled with an unpopular policy, Jefferson signed a law repealing the Embargo Act a few days before he left office.

Lewis and Clark expedition. In 1804 Jefferson commissioned his private secretary, Meriweather Lewis, to explore the territory acquired in the Louisiana Purchase. With William Clark, another Virginian wise in the ways of the frontier, Lewis led an expedition to the Pacific. The pair were to trace the Missouri River to its source, find a water route to the Pacific, and record the plant and animal life found along the way. With the Indian woman Sacajawea as their guide and interpreter, they crossed the Rockies and reached the Columbia River. In September of 1806 they returned to St. Louis to find that the country had given them up for lost.

Clark and Lewis

Choose the best answer.

2.1 *Marbury v. Madison* was the first of many important decisions made by this man during his thirty-five years as Chief Justice of the Supreme Court. _____
  a. Jefferson
  b. Marshall
  c. Adams
  d. Monroe

2.2 What was the price paid for the Louisiana Purchase? _____
  a. $5 million
  b. $15 million
  c. $10 million
  d. $20 million

2.3 "A wise and frugal government" was the goal that this man stated in his inaugural address. _____
  a. Madison
  b. Monroe
  c. Adams
  d. Jefferson

2.4 President Jefferson appointed this man as secretary of the treasury. _____
  a. Adams
  b. Pinckney
  c. Gallatin
  d. Madison

2.5 Jefferson's government was the beginning of _____ .
  a. a period of increased national debt and government spending
  b. a wise and popular government in the United States
  c. widespread removal of Federalist officeholders
  d. increased internal taxation

2.6 The practice by the British of impressing American seamen was brought to a head by the _____
  a. Lewis and Clark expedition.
  b. *Chesapeake* Affair.
  c. Embargo Act.
  d. American blockade.

2.7 The Embargo Act was an attempt to _____ .
  a. punish the southern states for seceding from the Union
  b. bring an end to the impressment of French seamen
  c. permanently damage the American economy
  d. exert pressure on England after the *Chesapeake* Affair

Fill in the blanks.

2.8 President Jefferson sent _____ to France to negotiate with Napoleon.

2.9 The two men who arranged the purchase of the Louisiana Territory were _____ and _____ .

True/False.

2.10 _____ Jefferson's term of office was not quite the "revolution" he later remembered.

2.11 _____ One of Jefferson's first acts as president was to release those who were still in jail as a result of disloyalty to the Federalist Party.

2.12 _____ Jefferson's aim, as stated in his inaugural address, was to let the people regulate their own pursuits of industry and profit.

2.13 _____ Napoleon's army captured the island of San Salvador, then moved on to occupy Louisiana and close the port of New Orleans.

2.14 _____ Napoleon was anxious to sell the Louisiana Territory because he needed money to continue his war with England.

THE WAR OF 1812

A Second War for Independence. James Madison came to the presidency at a crucial time. The struggle between Napoleon and Great Britain was reaching a climax, and neither side felt it could afford to respect the rights of neutrals. For three years, Madison pursued the Jeffersonian policy of economic boycott. Though he did not know it, the policy worked well against Great Britain. Parliament voted to lift its Orders in Council at the very time that Congress was voting a declaration of war against Britain.

The demand for war came in large part from the planters, small farmers, and frontiersmen of the American South and West. The motives of these men, who became known as "War Hawks," were mixed. They wanted to punish Britain for interfering with American trade and impressing American seamen. They also wanted to conquer Canada and Florida and to break British and Spanish ties with the Indians.

National Archives

James Madison

The War of 1812 brought none of the quick conquests predicted by the War Hawks. American efforts to invade Canada were unsuccessful. However, the American navy acquitted itself well, both on the inland lakes and at sea. At New Orleans the British suffered a crushing defeat at the hands of Andrew Jackson, a colorful frontier general who became a national hero because of this victory. The war ended with the Treaty of Ghent, which restored the prewar boundaries but said nothing about the causes of the conflict.

From the standpoint of American morale, the War of 1812 was a "Second War of Independence." Although ill-prepared for war, the United States held its own against the British army and navy. Americans proved to themselves—and to the world—that they could fight a great power. Wartime victories and increasing economic independence gave rise to a strong feeling of national pride and spurred efforts to establish an American culture.

Causes of the war. When Britain and France renewed warfare in 1803, the United States was caught squarely in the middle. England's Orders in Council stated that if neutral ships docked in ports controlled by France, they were no longer neutral. Napoleon, in turn, was intent on making sure that no British exports reached Europe. Both wanted to buy goods and foodstuffs from America. Also, the continued impressment of American sailors by the British and seizure of ships by France was of even greater concern to the United States. Nevertheless, American trade flourished during this time and merchants were willing to take the risk.

One of the methods used by the United States to try to persuade the British to change their policy toward neutral shipping was to place an embargo on all foreign ships coming into American ports and forbidding American ships to sail for any foreign ports. This policy, known as the Embargo Act of 1807, hurt no one but the American merchants. England and France remained unaffected and the Embargo Act was eventually repealed.

Of the two trade bills that were passed after the repeal of the Embargo Act, only one—the Macon Bill of 1810—actually helped American commerce. It also created major problems for the United States. Napoleon used the provisions of the Macon Bill to trap President Madison into cutting off trade with Britain. The bill stated that if either of the two nations—England or France—allowed free passage of American ships on the high seas, the United States would re-institute its no-trade policy against the non-compliant nation. Napoleon craftily stated, "His Majesty loves the Americans" and promised that French ships would no longer seize American ships and confiscate their cargo—a promise he had no intention of keeping.

President Madison sent word to the British parliament that if the Orders in Council were not repealed in three months' time, the United States would cut off trade with England. French ships, however, continued to seize American ships on the high seas. Fearing that America would lose credibility by changing its mind so many times, Madison refused to back down on his demands to Britain and in 1811, America stopped all trade and placed itself in open conflict with England.

25

Declaration of war. If the telegraph had existed during this time, the War of 1812 would probably never have occurred. On June 16, 1812, two days before war was declared, Britain announced that it would repeal its Orders in Council. Unfortunately, word of this action did not reach the United States until too late. Citing impressment, the continued British presence in the West, and the seizure of U.S. ships, Congress declared war.

The nation was divided in its support of the war against England. Northeastern manufacturers and shippers were adamantly opposed to the war because it would interfere with their business. Representatives from the West and South clamored for war for a number of reasons: (1) they wanted to punish England for interfering with American trade and impressing American seamen—national honor was at stake and needed to be defended; (2) they felt that the Indian attacks against U.S. troops and settlers in the North and West were, in large part, encouraged by the British; and (3) most significantly, they wanted to expand America's frontiers and enable the United States to become a great nation respected by the world. Because of their insistent cries for war, these frontier representatives were dubbed "War Hawks."

John C. Calhoun

John C. Calhoun of South Carolina (pictured) and Henry Clay of Kentucky were two War Hawk leaders who would for the next fifty years play a significant part in the shaping of America's destiny.

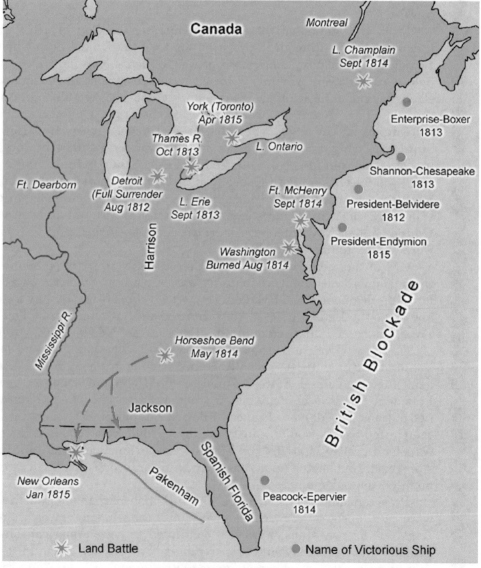

War of 1812

HISTORY & GEOGRAPHY

1 1 0 3

LIFEPAC TEST

$\dfrac{72}{90}$

Name _____

Date _____

Score _____

Choose one (each answer, 2 points).

1.   Washington's main objective as president of the United States was to _____
        a. maintain his power and get reelected.
        b. keep peace between the northern and southern states.
        c. establish respect for the office of the presidency.
        d. set up a court similar to that of European monarchs.

2.   Alexander Hamilton proposed paying the entire national debt at its face value in order to _____
        a. win the support of the congressmen who had speculated in government certificates.
        b. reimburse only the original holders of certificates who still possessed them.
        c. restore the nation's economic credit so that the government could raise money in the future.
        d. keep to a minimum the amount of money paid by the government.

3.   Jay's Treaty of 1794 _____
        a. provided that the British would stop interfering with American ships.
        b. provided that the British would stop impressing American seamen.
        c. prevented a war between England and the United States.
        d. allowed for the annexation of Canada by the United States.

4.   The Alien and Sedition Acts were designed to _____
        a. keep the number of foreign immigrants to the United States to a minimum.
        b. squelch the Republican opposition to the Federalist administration.
        c. make it easier for immigrants to become citizens.
        d. give formal recognition to the part system within the American government.

5.   One of the significant changes in atmosphere in Jefferson's administration was _____
        a. the closing of the Bank of the United States.
        b. the reduction of taxes and the trimming of government costs.
        c. the widespread dismissal of Federalist officeholders.
        d. the reinstatement of the Alien and Sedition Acts.

6.   The "War Hawks" were _____
        a. a flock of aggressive, predatory birds.
        b. representatives from the North who supported continued trading with Great Britain and war with France.
        c. frontiersmen and farmers of the West and South who wanted to expand America's frontiers.
        d. sailors who were victims of British impressment and wanted revenge.

7.   What did Jackson's unofficial cabinet became known as? _____
        a. "the parlor cabinet"
        b. "the kitchen cabinet"
        c. "the executive cabinet"
        d. "the White House cabinet"

8.   The Treaty of Ghent _____
        a. provided for the return to the United States of all impressed seamen.
        b. returned everything to the prewar status quo.
        c. opened ports of West Indies to United States trade.
        d. none of the above

9.   The period following the War of 1812 was called the "Era of Good Feelings" because _____
        a. the Republicans praised Marshall's decisions.
        b. Congress passed protective tariffs with widespread support.
        c. both parties buried their differences.
        d. all of the above.
        e. none of the above.

10. Which of the following was not a provision of the Monroe Doctrine? _____
a. America would not interfere in any foreign wars.
b. America would not interfere with existing colonies.
c. Dangerous immigrants to America be deported.
d. The Americas would not be considered open to colonization.
e. Any colonization attempts by foreign country would be considered a threat to peace.

11. Sectional differences were increased _____
a. as the Northeast developed into a strong industrial center.
b. when invention of the cotton gin made cotton more profitable.
c. when pioneers moved west and demanded internal improvements.
d. all of the above.
e. none of the above.

12. The controversy over Missouri's request for statehood _____
a. did not affect the balance of power in Congress.
b. was settled by the Missouri Compromise.
c. precipitated the Webster "Liberty and Union" speech.
d. all of the above.
e. none of the above.

Fill in the blanks (each answer, 3 points).

13. The two men who arranged the purchase of the Louisiana Territory were:
_____ and _____ .

True/False (each answer, 2 points).

14. _____ Although not specifically mentioned in the Constitution, the institution of a presidential cabinet was begun by Washington.

15. _____ The Constitution made provision for a Supreme Court but left the format of the court to Congress.

16. _____ Thomas Pickney's treaty with Spain won for the United States free navigation of the Mississippi and permission for American traders to deposit goods for shipment at the mouth of the river.

17. _____ When Washington said that the United States would be "friendly and impartial" in regard to foreign conflicts he was, in essence, saying that the United States would remain neutral.

18. _____ The XYZ Affair got its name because the American envoys refused to name the three English officials who demanded a large amount of money before they would even discuss a peace treaty.

19. _____ The Alien and Sedition Acts violated the First Amendment which guarantees freedom of speech and press.

20. _____ The Twelfth Amendment provides for the electors to cast separate ballots for president and for vice president.

21. _____ Jefferson's "Revolution of 1800" was not as much of a revolution as he thought.

22. _____ Jefferson's administration was the beginning of popular government in the United States.

23. _____ The *Marbury v. Madison* decision established the principle of federal control of interstate commerce.

24. _____ If there had been a telegraph, the War of 1812 would probably not have started.

25. _____ Many historians believe the leading motive for the War of 1812 was the western desire for land expansion.

26. _____ European countries did not test the Monroe Doctrine because of America's superior military strength.

27. _____ The Erie Canal shortened time but increased cost of sending products from the West to the East.

28. _____ The Panic of 1819 was due in part to the rapid expansion in industry and agriculture and to uncontrolled land speculation.

29. _____ Under Andrew Jackson the forces of nationalism and sectionalism were in continual conflict.

30. _____ The Battle of New Orleans was the final, decisive battle that won the War of 1812.

31. _____ Jackson's last years were plagued by financial troubles brought about by his fight against the national bank.

Match the following items (each answer, 2 points).

32. _____ Oliver Hazard Perry

a. a Federalist judge who wanted his commission granted

33. _____ Thomas MacDonough

b. witnessed the British bombardment of Fort McHenry

34. _____ John C. Calhoun and Henry Clay

c. War Hawks

35. _____ Francis Scott Key

d. sold the Louisiana Territory to United States

36. _____ John Marshall

e. won the Battle of Lake Erie

37. _____ James Madison

f. bought an empire instead of a city

38. _____ Napoleon

g. President Jefferson's secretary of the treasury

39. _____ Lewis and Clark

h. won the Battle of New Orleans against the British

40. _____ Albert Gallatin

i. first to declare act of Congress unconstitutional

41. _____ William Marbury

j. won the Battle of Lake Champlain

42. _____ Andrew Jackson

k. explored the Louisiana Territory and points west

43. _____ Monroe and Livingston

l. President Jefferson's secretary of state

Unprepared for war. Even though many Americans were in favor of war, the nation was ill-prepared to fight. President Jefferson's frugal economic policies had been good for the national economy but were harmful for national defense. During his term, Jefferson had drastically reduced the size of the army and had sold most of the navy's vessels. At the time war was declared against England, there were fewer than 7,000 soldiers—most poorly trained—and the navy had less than twenty warships. In addition, some New England states refused to allow their state militias to be released for national duty, and bankers in the Northeast refused to make loans to help finance the war effort. Some New England merchants even continued to trade with Canada and the British fleet during the war!

Battles of the war. The early battles of the war were directed unsuccessfully against Canada. Instead of a concentrated attack on the small British force in Canada (which probably would have been successful), American armies attempted a three-pronged assault. These attacks were ineffective and were driven back, in large part, by Indian tribes who sided with the British in hopes of seeing the Americans driven from Indian lands. Detroit and Ft. Dearborn were lost to the combined British and Indian forces, and American troops were driven out of the Northwest Territory.

The Battle of Lake Erie in 1813 was fought by Captain Oliver Hazard Perry and proved to be the turning point for the Americans in regaining the Northwest. Led by Captain Perry, Americans quickly built an improvised fleet of ships and defeated the superior British forces on Lake Erie. Control of Lake Erie led to the defeat of the British in Detroit and placed the Northwest Territory under American control once again.

The Americans made a final, abortive attempt to invade Canada in 1814. A few successful skirmishes against the British were offset by an indecisive battle at Lundy's Lane in which the Americans were forced to withdraw across the border. By this time, Britain had defeated Napoleon and was ready to concentrate her efforts on winning the war against the United States. In the fall of 1814, the British sent 11,000 troops down Lake Champlain to attack the western portion of New York. Led by Captain Thomas MacDonough, the Americans defeated the British on Lake Champlain and forced the invasion back into Canada. Further American attempts to invade Canada were abandoned.

Probably the most embarrassing defeat for the Americans was the capture and burning of Washington, D.C. by the British in 1814. British ships sailed into Chesapeake Bay, landed in Maryland, and marched inland toward Washington, D.C. The 6,000 hastily-assembled American recruits were no match for the British troops, who marched unopposed into the city. President Madison and his wife, Dolley, hurriedly packed important government papers and a portrait of George Washington and fled the White House. The British troops marched in and torched the Capitol, the White House, and other public buildings, then abandoned the city.

Dolley Madison   The invasion of Washington, D.C. was offset by a subsequent, stirring naval battle in which the British sailed on up the Chesapeake, intent on destroying Fort McHenry at the entrance of Baltimore's harbor. Although they bombarded the fort all night, the next morning the American flag was still waving proudly over the fort. Francis Scott Key was being detained on board one of the British vessels and witnessed the entire battle. The sight of the American flag still flying by "dawn's early light" inspired Key to write "The Star-Spangled Banner."

Instead of demoralizing the Americans as the British had intended, the burning of Washington, D.C. served to unite citizens of the United States, and thousands volunteered for military service. As a result, England decided to move its offensive south to the Gulf Coast.

The Battle of New Orleans, fought on January 8, 1815, was the last engagement of the war. Had communication been swifter, this battle could probably have been prevented. A peace treaty had been signed on December 24, 1814 at Ghent, Belgium—fifteen days before the Battle of New Orleans took place. However, word had not yet reached the United States. Andrew Jackson and Jean Laffite, with their rag-tag army of 4,500 frontiersmen and pirates, went head to head against the highly-disciplined redcoats commanded by General Edward Pakenham. Pakenham was sure when the volunteers saw the formidable ranks of British soldiers advancing, they would bolt in terror. On the contrary, the Americans stood their ground. Those redcoats that were not killed by artillery fire were methodically mowed down by Jackson's sharpshooting riflemen. Some 2,100 British soldiers were killed or wounded within the course of half an hour. Pakenham was killed in the battle, and a surviving British officer called a retreat of the remaining British troops.

Andrew Jackson

End of the war. Both Great Britain and the United States were becoming war-weary. The economy of both nations had suffered. England's economy suffered because of the expense of fighting a war first with France then with America. The British blockade of American trading ships had severely damaged the economy of the United States.

In the summer of 1814, an American delegation consisting of Henry Clay, John Quincy Adams, Albert Gallatin, James A. Bayard, and Jonathan Russell was sent to Ghent, Belgium to negotiate peace with England. The resultant treaty, signed in December of 1814, was nothing more than a cease-fire. No territory was lost or gained, all boundaries were restored exactly as they were before war was declared, and neither the British impressments and blockades nor the British Orders in Council were addressed in the treaty. The two nations simply agreed to stop fighting.

Henry Clay

Results of the war. In spite of its apparent lack of success in the War of 1812, America did benefit in several ways. First, America gained the respect of foreign nations by proving to the world that it could take a stand against England, the acknowledged ruler of the seas. Second, when imported manufactured goods were no longer available because of the British blockade of American ships, American industry was forced to produce its own products. Third, Americans were proud of their efforts during the war, and a new spirit of nationalism was created. Fourth, America was now ready to expand westward because Indian hostilities had, for the time being, been successfully crushed, and the British finally surrendered their forts.

The Star-Spangled Banner

Oh! say, can you see by the dawn's early light,
What so proudly we hailed at the twilight's last gleaming?
Whose broad stripes and bright stars, through the perilous fight,
O'er the ramparts we watched were so gallantly streaming?
And the rocket's red glare, the bombs bursting in air,
Gave proof through the night that our flag was still there.
Oh! say, does that Star-Spangled Banner yet wave
O'er the land of the free and the home of the brave?

On the shore, dimly seen through the mists of the deep,
Where the foe's haughty host in dread silence reposes,
What is that which the breeze, o'er the towering steep,
As it fitfully blows, half conceals, half discloses?
Now it catches the gleam of the morning's first beam,
In full glory reflected, now shines on the stream.
'Tis the Star-Spangled Banner, Oh! long may it wave
O'er the land of the free and the home of the brave!

And where is that band who so vauntingly swore
That the havoc of war and the battle's confusion
A home and a country should leave us no more?
Their blood has washed out their foul footstep's pollution.
No refuge could save the hireling and slave
From the terror of flight or the gloom of the grave,
And the Star-Spangled Banner in triumph doth wave
O'er the land of the free and the home of the brave.

Oh! thus be it ever when freemen shall stand
Between their lov'd home and the war's desolation,
Blest with vict'ry and peace, may the heav'n-rescued land
Praise the power that hath made and preserved us a nation.
Then conquer we must, when our cause it is just,
And this be our motto- "In God is our trust."
And the Star-Spangled Banner in triumph shall wave
O'er the land of the free and the home of the brave.

Choose one.

2.15   The "War Hawks" were _____
    a. a flock of aggressive, predatory birds.
    b. representatives from the North who supported continued trading with Great Britain and war with France.
    c. frontiersmen and farmers of the West and South who wanted to expand America's frontiers.
    d. sailors who were victims of British impressment and wanted revenge.

2.16   Britain and France _____
    a. were at war with each other but supported the shipping rights of neutral nations.
    b. were greatly affected by the Embargo Act of 1807.
    c. seized American ships.
    d. tried to negotiate a peaceful settlement of their differences.

True/False.

2.17   _____ Had the telegraph been in existence, the War of 1812 might never have occurred.

2.18   _____ Napoleon trapped President Madison into cutting off trade with Britain.

2.19   _____ The Embargo Act of 1807 was an effective tool in persuading England to change its policy toward neutral shipping.

2.20   _____ The Macon Bill of 1810 was unsuccessful in helping American commerce.

2.21   _____ The Battle of New Orleans was the final, decisive battle that won the War of 1812.

2.22   _____ The United States was poorly prepared for war because of the economic policies of James Madison.

2.23   _____ The burning of Washington, D.C. by the British was an attempt to boost American morale.

2.24   _____ The American army was unsuccessful in its attempt to drive the British out of Canada.

Match the following items.

2.25   _____ Battle of Lake Erie   a. Andrew Jackson

2.26   _____ Battle of New Orleans   b. John C. Calhoun and Henry Clay

2.27   _____ Battle of Lake Champlain   c. Thomas MacDonough

2.28   _____ War Hawks   d. Francis Scott Key

2.29   _____ "Star-Spangled Banner"   e. Oliver Hazard Perry

Fill in the blanks.

2.30   A peace treaty was signed in Ghent, Belgium _____ days before the Battle of New Orleans.

2.31   The "Star-Spangled Banner" was inspired by the night-long bombardment of Fort _____ by British ships.

Answer the following questions.

2.32   List four ways in which the United States benefited from the War of 1812.

        1. _____
           _____

        2. _____
           _____

        3. _____
           _____

        4. _____
           _____

2.33   What were the terms of the Treaty of Ghent?

        _____
        _____
        _____
        _____

Adult Check   _____
                   Initial   Date

Review the material in this section in preparation for the Self Test. The Self Test will check your mastery of this particular section. The items missed on this Self Test will indicate specific areas where restudy is needed for mastery.

SELF TEST 2

Choose one (each answer, 2 points).

2.01   The Embargo Act of 1807 _____
    a. was Jefferson's attempt to keep the country at peace and avoid further provocative incidents.
    b. stopped the export of American goods and prohibited all U.S. ships from leaving for foreign ports.
    c. was denounced by New England merchants and western and southern farmers alike.
    d. all of the above.

2.02   The declaration of war in 1812 was strongly opposed by _____ .
    a. New England merchants
    b. the War Hawks
    c. western farmers
    d. southern Republicans

2.03   Which of the following does *not* describe the state of the country's preparedness for the War of 1812? _____
    a. The United States had an ocean-going navy of fewer than twenty vessels.
    b. The army was small and the men were poorly trained.
    c. Congress' efforts to raise money for the war were thwarted by the minority that was against the war.
    d. Loyal Americans were eager to give up their civilian jobs to volunteer to fight for the cause of their nation.

2.04   Which of the following was a notable British victory in the War of 1812? _____
    a. the capture and burning of Washington, D.C.
    b. the battle of New Orleans
    c. the battle of Lake Erie
    d. the capture of Pensacola

2.05   Andrew Jackson _____
    a. successfully captured Montreal from the British in 1813.
    b. won the battle of New Orleans from the British.
    c. represented the United States in the peace negotiations at Ghent, Belgium.
    d. all of the above.

2.06   New Englanders persistently defied the American cause in the war by _____
    a. refusing to release their militias for national duty.
    b. boycotting government loans.
    c. continuing to trade with Canada and furnishing supplies to the British fleet.
    d. all of the above.

2.07   The Treaty of Ghent represented _____
    a. a substantial victory for the United States.
    b. a substantial victory for the British.
    c. a return to conditions as they were prior to the war.
    d. a diplomatic coup for Napoleon.

True/False (each answer, 2 points).

2.08   _____   During Jefferson's term in office the power of the Supreme Court was increased.

2.09   _____   Jefferson's administration was the beginning of popular government in the United States.

2.010 _____ The Embargo Act of 1807 did serious damage to the economies of England and France.

2.011 _____ The British navy needed sailors and began taking them off American vessels by force in a procedure called impressment.

2.012 _____ The Battle of New Orleans was the final, decisive battle that won the War of 1812.

2.013 _____ An indirect source of the crisis that led to the War of 1812 was the constant demand for more and more land by southern and western expansionists.

2.014 _____ The initial campaign of the Americans in 1812—to invade and conquer Canada—was their first victory in the war.

Match these items (each answer, 2 points).

2.015 _____ John Marshall   a. won the Battle of Lake Erie

2.016 _____ Thomas Jefferson   b. War Hawks

2.017 _____ James Madison   c. a Federalist judge who wanted his commission granted

2.018 _____ Napoleon   d. led "Revolution of 1800"

2.019 _____ Lewis and Clark   e. sold Louisiana Territory to United States

2.020 _____ Francis Scott Key   f. won the Battle of New Orleans against the British

2.021 _____ Albert Gallatin   g. bought an empire instead of a city

2.022 _____ William Marbury   h. first to declare act of Congress unconstitutional

2.023 _____ Andrew Jackson   i. President Jefferson's secretary of the treasury

2.024 _____ Calhoun and Clay   j. witnessed the bombardment of Fort McHenry

2.025 _____ Oliver Hazard Perry   k. President Jefferson's secretary of state

2.026 _____ Monroe and Livingston l. explored the Louisiana Territory and points west

Answer the following question (each answer, 5 points).

2.027 What were the terms of the Treaty of Ghent?

_____

_____

_____

_____

_____

46 / 57

Score
Adult Check

_____

Initial   Date

III. NATIONALISM AND SECTIONALISM

Following the War of 1812, America's attention turned inward. Years of involvement in international affairs were followed by years of nationalism in which many Americans were absorbed mainly with several national issues. Much of the pressing business before the nation was related in one way or another to sectional points of view—to **sectionalism**.

By the 1820s, real sectional differences had surfaced within the United States. Citizens in different parts of the nation often had strongly clashing political, social, and economic interests. These differences resulted in lively political controversies and disputes, sometimes posing a serious threat to national unity.

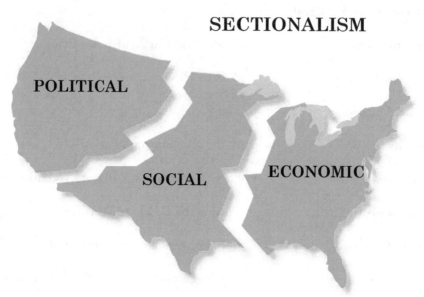

One of the most serious sectional disputes arose over the question of slavery. Should new states admitted to the Union be allowed to decide for themselves whether they were "slave" or "free"? This issue was resolved temporarily by the Missouri Compromise. In this agreement, an imaginary line was drawn at the thirty-sixth parallel, dividing future slave states from future free states within the remaining territory of the Louisiana Purchase. However, the challenge to slavery that had prompted the Compromise left a legacy of ill feeling between North and South.

Southerners and westerners also differed from northerners in their opposition to high tariffs and to the policies of the Bank of the United States—both of which benefited the northern manufacturers.

The extension of suffrage during this period contributed to the liveliness of the American political scene. The number of voters swelled as states extended the right to vote to nearly all adult white males.

SECTION OBJECTIVES

Review these objectives. When you have completed this section, you should be able to:

11. Describe the ways in which Chief Justice John Marshall's rulings established precedents for national supremacy over states' rights and define the roles of the Court and Congress.

12. Explain the provisions of the Monroe Doctrine.

13. Identify the factors encouraging western migration after 1820 and indicate the ways in which the rising importance of the west influenced the social, economic, and political trends of the rest of the country.

14. Discuss the role of slavery and economic depression in ending the "Era of Good Feelings" and precipitating a revival of sectional and political strife.

15. Cite factors that gave the common man new status during the Jacksonian era.

16. Describe the major characteristics of the two-party system during the Jacksonian era.

17. Trace the relationship between Jackson's view of the presidency and Thomas Jefferson's view and show how circumstances forced Jackson, like his predecessor, to support an activist federal government.

18. Describe the factions for and against the National Bank during the 1830s and the bank's role in the nation's history.

VOCABULARY

Study these words to enhance your learning success in this section.

Monroe Doctrine – The doctrine that European nations should not interfere with American nations or try to acquire more territory in the Western Hemisphere; came from President Monroe's message in Congress on December 2, 1823 and became a part of United States foreign policy

sectionalism – Too great a regard for sectional interests; sectional prejudice or hatred

inflation – A sharp sudden rise in prices resulting in a too great expansion in paper money or bank credit

nullify – To make void

speculation – Buying or selling when there is a large risk with the hopes of making a profit from future price changes

squatter – A person who settles on land without title or right

spoils system – The system or practice in which public offices were awarded to supporters of the winning party

wildcat bank – Prior to 1863-64, a bank operation with insufficient capital to redeem its circulating notes

Among the factors that promoted the growth of nationalism were the far-reaching decisions of the Supreme Court under John Marshall. Surprisingly, many Republicans praised Marshall's decisions. Furthermore, as the fear of the central government waned, the Republican Party adopted a number of Federalist principles. Without much debate, Republicans in Congress passed a protective tariff, established a second national bank, and reached a diplomatic understanding with Britain. Indeed, the Republicans acted so much like the Federalists that the two parties buried their differences during what was termed the "Era of Good Feelings."

Just beneath this placid surface ran strong currents of sectionalism. The special economic interests of the Northeast, the West, and the South led to political differences on the major issues of the day—the bank, the tariff, internal improvements, and slavery. During the 1820s, these political differences wrought the formation once again of two distinct political parties. The nationalistic spirit of 1815 gave way to sectional rivalry by 1828.

NATIONALISM AND THE MONROE ADMINISTRATION

President Monroe, who succeeded James Madison in the White House, frequently referred in his speeches to the new national feeling that swept the country in the years after the War of 1812. In his inaugural address he stated that "increased harmony of opinion" had developed. In his first annual message to Congress, he rejoiced that "local jealousies are rapidly yielding to more generous, enlarged and enlightened views of national policy."

The "Era of Good Feelings." James Monroe, Madison's secretary of state, was elected president in 1816. During his first term he adopted enough of the Federalist principles to satisfy former Federalists. In the election of 1820, Monroe received all but one electoral vote. With that, the Federalist Party died out, and no new opposition party arose. Monroe toured the country—something no other president had done. In New England an article was published entitled "Era of Good Feelings," a name that has been used by historians to describe this period.

James Monroe

During the War of 1812, American manufacturers were forced to produce the materials needed within the United States. Following the war, England deluged the American market with goods that were priced much lower than those of the budding American manufacturers, hoping to regain their markets. Many American manufacturers went into bankruptcy. Of the one hundred fifty textile mills around Providence, Rhode Island, fewer than a dozen survived.

Manufacturers asked Congress for a protective tariff. Even Thomas Jefferson, who had once urged that "our work-shops remain in Europe," admitted at the end of the war that "manufacturers are now as necessary to our independence as to our comfort. We must now place the manufacturer by the side of the agriculturist."

In 1816 Congress passed a tariff that raised the duties on many imported articles. Daniel Webster of Massachusetts spoke against the tariff because New England profited from the brisk trade with England. John C. Calhoun of South Carolina argued for the Tariff of 1816 as a national necessity.

Although the South did not yet have many industries, they had the raw materials, water power, and manpower; and they confidently expected that soon they would have textile factories that would benefit from the tariff. Within a decade, both Webster and Calhoun would change their views. In New England manufacturing would outweigh commercial interests. In the South the dreams of industrialization would be abandoned.

Daniel Webster

The influence of John Marshall. The opinions of Chief Justice John Marshall strengthened national government during this period. Marshall served as Chief Justice of the Supreme Court from 1801 to 1835 and personally wrote more than five hundred decisions. In vigorous prose and with clear logic, he translated his nationalistic views into law. To him, the Supreme Court was more than a court—it was a platform from which he could proclaim to the nation those principles that gave life to the Constitution. In his decisions, Marshall accomplished two important things. First, by a broad interpretation of the Constitution, he strengthened the federal government at the expense of the states. Second, through his energy and vigor, the Supreme Court gained an importance in the federal government that it retains to this day.

Andrew Jackson

The military victory of Andrew Jackson. After the War of 1812, Spain began to have difficulty controlling the Indians in Florida. When the Seminoles and the Creeks were encouraged by a British colonel to raid American territory, Andrew Jackson was sent to Florida with orders to adopt "necessary measures." In 1818 he and his men swept into Florida, captured Pensacola from the Spaniards, and claimed the surrounding territory for the United States. Spain could not establish effective control over Florida and eventually ceded Florida by treaty to the United States in return for payment of claims that American citizens held against Spain in the amount of $5 million.

The Monroe Doctrine. Seeing the plight of Spain, Britain proposed joint British-American action to stop other European countries from establishing colonies in the Americas. Secretary of State John Quincy Adams opposed this plan because he thought the United States should act independently.

Following Adams' advice, Monroe announced a new policy in his annual message to Congress in December of 1823. This statement, known as the **Monroe Doctrine**, was a landmark in United States history. The important points of the Monroe Doctrine were these: (1) that the United States would not take part in any foreign wars; (2) the United States would not interfere with any existing European colonies; (3) the American continents were not subject to future colonization by European powers; and (4) any attempt by European powers to further colonize the United States would be considered a threat to America's peace and safety. The first part of the document was a pledge that America would stay out of European affairs that did not concern the United States, and it would not interfere with existing European colonies in the Americas. The second part was a warning to European nations to maintain a "hands off" position in relation to the Western Hemisphere.

The European countries, however, considered the Monroe Doctrine to be unimportant. The president's desire to guard the Western Hemisphere was somewhat ridiculous in view of America's weak military position. However, knowing that the British navy would back up the Monroe Doctrine, they made no attempt to restore Spain's New World empire, and Spain finally recognized the independence of her American colonies. In 1824 Russia agreed to establish the southern boundary of Alaska at 54° 40'. Consequently, the Doctrine was never really tested in this early period. Its real importance would come years later when it would become a cornerstone of American foreign policy.

The westward movement. The War of 1812 was scarcely over when the westward movement began. The Indians had been pacified and fertile land was available. Travel was difficult, however, and many travelers became ill on the frontier. One Englishman observed these ailing pioneers and wondered why they endured the "rugged road, the dirty hovels, the fire in the woods to sleep by, the pathless ways through the wilderness, and the dangerous crossings of the rivers." The answer was the chance to buy cheap, fertile land and the opportunity to begin a new life in the West.

Four new states were admitted to the Union shortly after the War of 1812: Indiana, Mississippi, Illinois, and Alabama. Vermont, Ohio, Kentucky, and Tennessee had previously joined the Union. Westerners soon found a need for better transportation. Farmers harvested crops that exceeded their local needs and were looking for markets. Sending products back over the turnpikes to the East was too expensive. Shipping them down the Mississippi to New Orleans and from there to the eastern ports took too long.

In 1817 DeWitt Clinton persuaded the New York state legislature to authorize the building of a canal between the Hudson River and Lake Erie. Clinton's proposed canal would connect Albany and Buffalo, a distance of 363 miles, and would cost seven million dollars. The project seemed so preposterous that it was sarcastically called "Clinton's Big Ditch." However, the canal was completed in 1825, and freight rates between Buffalo and Albany dropped 90 percent per ton. Travel time was cut from 20 days to 8 days. So heavy was the traffic on the Erie Canal that it paid for itself within nine years. Other states followed New York's example and built canals to carry their products to market.

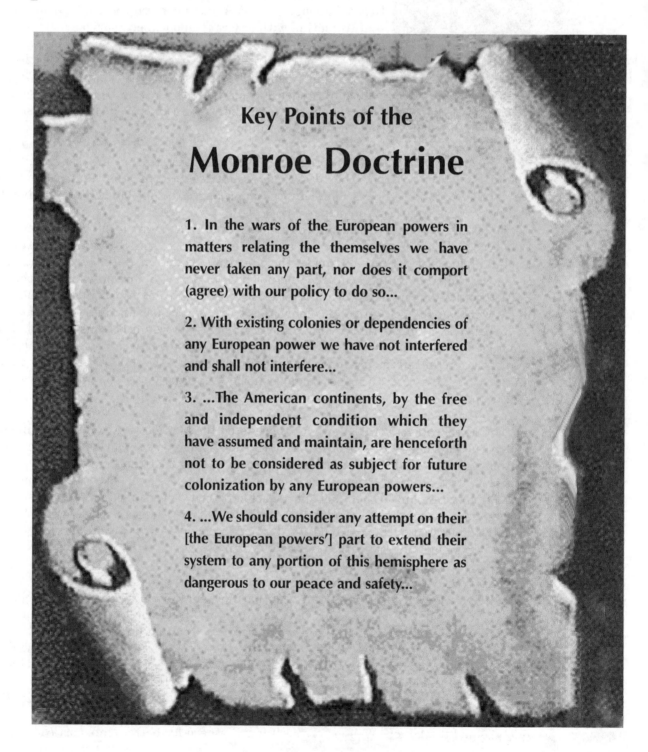

Key Points of the
Monroe Doctrine

1. In the wars of the European powers in matters relating the themselves we have never taken any part, nor does it comport (agree) with our policy to do so...

2. With existing colonies or dependencies of any European power we have not interfered and shall not interfere...

3. ...The American continents, by the free and independent condition which they have assumed and maintain, are henceforth not to be considered as subject for future colonization by any European powers...

4. ...We should consider any attempt on their [the European powers'] part to extend their system to any portion of this hemisphere as dangerous to our peace and safety...

Fill in the blanks.

3.1   The policy that European nations should not interfere with America was known
       as the _____ .

3.2   The power of the federal government increased at the expense of the states because
       of far-reaching decisions of the _____ .

3.3   The _____ sought to regain their market for manufacturers
       in America by reducing the cost of their goods.

3.4   Many struggling American industries declared _____ .

3.5   Two broad goals achieved by the decisions written by Marshall were strengthening
       of the _____ and the establishing the importance of the
       _____ .

3.6   The United States acquired Florida from Spain by _____ .

3.7   The European powers viewed the Monroe Doctrine at that time as
       _____ .

3.8   The settlers in the West did not want to send their produce back to the East over the
       expensive _____ .

3.9   The Erie Canal cut the travel time between Buffalo and Albany from 20 days to
       _____ days and reduced freight rates by _____
       per ton.

Answer the following question.

3.10   List four points made in the Monroe Doctrine.

       _____

       _____

       _____

       _____

       _____

       _____

Choose the best answer(s).

3.11   More settlers moved westward after the War of 1812 because: _____ , _____ .
       a. more jobs were available out West
       b. there was plenty of cheap land
       c. the Indians had been brought under control
       d. travel to the West was easy

Match these men with their accomplishments.

3.12 _____ James Monroe a. succeeded James Madison as president

3.13 _____ Daniel Webster b. proposed construction of the Erie Canal

3.14 _____ Andrew Jackson c. opposed the Tariff of 1816

3.15 _____ DeWitt Clinton d. strengthened the influence of the Supreme Court

3.16 _____ John Marshall e. pushed Spain to cede Florida to the U.S.

3.17 _____ John C. Calhoun f. the secretary of state who supported the Monroe Doctrine

3.18 _____ John Quincy Adams g. supported the Tariff of 1816

SECTIONALISM AND THE JACKSON ADMINISTRATION

Even though the "Era of Good Feelings" seemed to be harmonious, sectional differences arose. People living in the Northeast, the South, and the West were developing their own attitudes and viewpoints. These differences developed from the special economic concerns of each section and the efforts of politicians to pass legislation in Congress that favored each section's concerns. From the 1820s to the 1860s, sectional rivalry was pitted against the spirit of nationalism.

In 1828 Andrew Jackson was elected to the presidency. As the acknowledged champion of the common people, Jackson acted to broaden participation in the federal government and to reduce the power of the Bank of the United States. He also initiated many important changes in the nature of American politics. Through the **spoils system,** he began the practice of rewarding political supporters with government jobs. He was also the first president to have two cabinets—an official cabinet and an unofficial "kitchen cabinet" of informal political advisers.

In addition, Jackson was largely responsible for the creation of two new political parties. Those who supported him in the election of 1824 started the Democratic Party. Those who opposed his chosen successor, Martin Van Buren, in the election of 1836 formed the Whig Party. In 1840 the Whig Party elected its first president, William Henry Harrison.

Sectionalism points of view. The Northeast was developing into a strong industrial center. Manufacturers wanted higher tariffs and favored the national bank because it kept the currency stable. They were lukewarm to westward expansion because it would remove men from their labor supply and reduce their influence in Congress as new states were added to the Union. They generally opposed internal improvements in the West because they would encourage expansion. They also opposed the spread of slavery, not so much for moral reasons at that time but because slave states would not support the tariff.

The South developed a different point of view on tariffs and internal improvements. The invention of Eli Whitney's cotton gin in 1793 made possible the rapid processing of large cotton crops. Cultivation of cotton had spread through the piedmont region of the South and along the Gulf Coast. Because cotton was profitable, the South poured money into it rather than into manufacturing. Since southerners needed to import goods, they preferred low protective tariffs. They favored western expansion in opposition to other sections because they needed new lands, but they insisted on taking their slaves with them. They were not in favor of internal improvements because their broad, navigable rivers met their transportation needs.

The West had a third point of view. As a farming area in need of markets, it favored a policy that made land available on easy terms and financed the construction of roads and canals. Some western cities supported the protective tariff. Westerners also supported the Bank of the United States until it changed its policy, and loans for land purchases were no longer easily obtained.

Panic of 1819

In 1819 a "panic," or depression, swept the country due, in part, to the rapid expansion of American manufacturing during the War of 1812 and the distress caused by the postwar British competition. The rapid expansion of American farming was another factor. Surplus farm products had been sold in Europe immediately after the war, but when European agriculture recovered, the demand for American goods declined and prices fell. Still another cause of the crisis was land **speculation** in the West. Thousands of settlers had purchased land on credit in the postwar years, and many of the land deals were financed by "**wildcat banks**." These state banks, like the national bank, were eager to lend money. However, land speculation was out of control by the latter part of 1818, and the directors of the national bank began to ask for repayment of their loans.

This tightening of credit and a sharp fall in farm prices touched off the Panic of 1819. Prices plummeted. In some places wheat fell from two dollars a bushel to twenty-five cents, and cotton dropped from thirty-three cents a pound to ten cents. Factories closed their doors, and thousands of people were thrown out of work. Western farmers who had taken land on credit could not repay their loans, and the banks foreclosed on their property.

During the depression that followed this panic, many "wildcat banks" were taken over by the Bank of the United States. So much land in the West and the Southwest fell into the hands of the national bank that it was said: "The bank was saved and the people were ruined." Politicians assailed the national bank as "the Monster" and blamed it for the country's troubles. Congress aided the westerners with a new Land Act in 1820. The act made possible the purchase of an 80-acre farm for only one hundred dollars, but cash payment was required. Even after prosperity returned, most westerners continued to distrust the national bank and the eastern financiers who ran it.

Missouri Compromise of 1820. Missouri's request for statehood sparked a controversy. When Missouri asked for statehood, the United States had eleven free states and eleven slave states. In the Senate, the North and the South had equal voting strength, but in the House the North had the greater strength because of its larger population. Although some mention was made of the moral aspect of slavery, most of the debate concerned political and constitutional issues. Southerners insisted that Congress had no constitutional right to decide whether a state was to be slave or free. The North insisted that Congress did have that right. The "momentous question" raised in the Missouri debate deeply disturbed Thomas Jefferson. It shattered the peace of the nation, he said, "like a fire bell in the night."

Fortunately, while the debate was going on, the northeastern counties of Massachusetts asked to be admitted to the Union as a separate state to be called Maine. The compromise of 1820, brokered by Henry Clay, allowed Missouri to be admitted as a slave state and Maine to be admitted as a free state. It declared that in the rest of the Louisiana Purchase territory, no slave states were to be admitted north of the parallel 36° 30'. The compromise calmed the political situation for the time being, but as John Quincy Adams warned, "the present question is a mere preamble—a title-page to a great, tragic volume."

Election of 1824. The Election of 1824 was a sectional contest. All the candidates called themselves Republicans, but their viewpoints differed. Four men ran for president: William H. Crawford from the South; John Quincy Adams from the Northeast; and Henry Clay and Andrew Jackson (pictured at left) from the West. When the votes were counted, Jackson led with Adams, Crawford, and Clay following in that order. Since no candidate had a majority, the vote on the top three—Jackson, Crawford, and Adams—went to the House of Representatives. Clay, as Speaker of the House, could aid any of the candidates. He opposed Jackson, his political rival in the West. Though he and Adams were different in personality

Andrew Jackson

and background, they agreed on several issues. Both favored a protective tariff, internal improvements, and the national bank. For these reasons, Clay gave his support to Adams, who was elected by the House in February of 1825. Adams promptly named Henry Clay as his secretary of state, a job that was viewed as a stepping stone to the presidency.

Adams' administration was plagued by the "corrupt bargain" charge that he had bought Clay's backing by promising him the position of secretary of state. His quarrels with Congress came to a head in 1828 with the "Tariff of Abominations," a tariff on raw materials and manufactured goods proposed by Jackson's supporters to discredit Adams. They believed their tariff was so high that all sections of the country would oppose it. John Randolph quite rightly charged that the tariff bill was concerned with "manufactures of no sort, but the manufacturing of a president of the United States." The elaborate scheme failed, for distasteful as the bill was, enough New Englanders voted that it passed both houses and was signed into law. Daniel Webster later explained: "Its enemies spiced it with whatsoever they thought would make it distasteful; its friends took it, drugged as it was." Out of the protests that followed, new political parties took shape. The Adams-Clay men called themselves National Republicans because they favored a nationalistic program. The Jackson followers called themselves Democrats. In 1828 Jackson led the Democrats to victory.

Complete the vocabulary matching.

3.19	_____ inflation	a.	a person who settles on land without title or right.
3.20	_____ nullify	b.	a sharp sudden rise in prices resulting in a too great expansion in paper money or bank credit.
3.21	_____ speculation	c.	buying or selling when there is a large risk with the hopes of making a profit from future price changes.
3.22	_____ squatter	d.	the system or practice in which public offices were awarded to supporters of the winning party.
3.23	_____ spoils system	e.	to make void
3.24	_____ wildcat bank	f.	prior to 1863-64, a bank operation with insufficient capital to redeem its circulating notes.

Match the following. Pick the two best answers for each section.

3.25	_____ , _____ South	a.	favored western expansion with slavery
3.26	_____ , _____ West	b.	favored the national bank
		c.	wanted financing for roads and canals
3.27	_____ , _____ Northeast	d.	wanted land available on easy terms
		e.	preferred low protective tariffs
		f.	wanted higher tariffs

True/False.

3.28 _____ The Panic of 1819 resulted partly from the rapid expansion of American manufacturing during the War of 1812 and the stress of postwar British competition.

3.29 _____ The tightening of credit and a sharp decrease in farm prices touched off the Panic of 1819.

3.30 _____ The national bank provided financing for western farmers to pay state banks for land taken on credit.

3.31 _____ Missouri's request for statehood led to controversy.

3.32 _____ Missouri was admitted as a "free" state.

3.33 _____ Since no candidate received a majority in the election of 1824, the vote on the top three went to the Senate.

3.34 _____ With the support of Henry Clay, John Quincy Adams was elected as president.

Fill in the blanks.

3.35 The election of 1824 was a _____ contest.

3.36 The four men who ran for president in 1824 were:

_____

_____

_____

_____

3.37 The two political parties that had evolved by 1828 were the

_____ and _____ .

3.38 Following the Panic of 1819, people in the West referred to the national bank as the

" _____ ."

Era of Jackson. During his eight years in the White House, Jackson was a colorful, vigorous, and controversial leader. Although the National Republicans disliked him intensely, the Democrats idolized him, and Jackson's political strength rested on the solid support of the people.

Throughout the Jacksonian Era the forces of sectionalism and nationalism were in conflict. Jackson sympathized with the states' rights argument, and he shared many of the sectional feelings of the West. Yet neither Jackson nor his successor Van Buren endangered the welfare of the Union by yielding to extreme sectional demands. When South Carolinians tried to **nullify** a tariff act, Jackson asserted the federal government's power. When he detected what he thought were special privileges for the second national bank, he refused to renew its charter. Sectionalism made some headway in the 1830s, but the course of national reform managed to hold it in check.

The Rise of Sectionalism

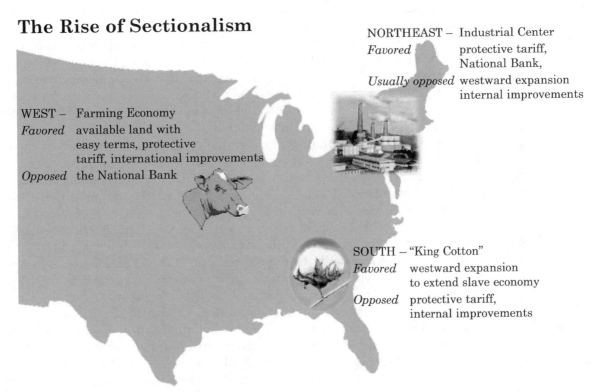

NORTHEAST – Industrial Center
Favored   protective tariff,
                 National Bank,
Usually opposed westward expansion
                 internal improvements

WEST –   Farming Economy
Favored   available land with
            easy terms, protective
            tariff, international improvements
Opposed   the National Bank

SOUTH – "King Cotton"
Favored   westward expansion
             to extend slave economy
Opposed   protective tariff,
             internal improvements

Jacksonian democracy drew upon Jefferson's political philosophy. Jefferson and his followers had promised the American people a share in the federal government. They believed that more people should have the right to vote, and they respected the political wisdom of humble men—particularly the farmers. Once in office, however, they had accomplished little in this direction. Instead, Jackson himself, coming from humble origins, opened new opportunities—educational, economic, and political—to the American people. This democratic upsurge rested upon the Jeffersonian belief in the worth of the individual. The impartial worth of the individual is a basic teaching of God's Word (Romans 2:11 and John 3:16).

One of the most important political changes in the Jacksonian Era was the extension of suffrage. Most of the original states had instituted property requirements and religious qualifications for voters. By 1840, so many states had liberalized their voting requirements that practically all free white men in the country—other than criminals—could vote.

Laborers and artisans were quick to use their newly-won political power and took a keen interest in politics. They banded together in working-men's parties calling for publicly-supported schools, shorter hours, abolition of compulsory militia duty, and revision of laws that imprisoned debtors. Laws were passed to improve working conditions in factories as well.

Jackson's inauguration was a triumph for democracy and people came great distances for the inauguration. Daniel Webster predicted, however, that the Democratic coalition that had put Jackson in the White House would be unable to keep him there long. Had the president been a less skillful politician, his winning coalition of 1828 might indeed have been smashed by his opponents in the election of 1832. His supporters had no common purpose to hold them together, and they were divided on many crucial issues. All, however, expected to share in the government, and through government patronage Jackson was able to hold these men with divided viewpoints together.

Jackson believed that the appointment of new men to government jobs by the incoming president was healthy. He was not a corrupt politician, and he removed only about one-sixth of all the government officeholders. Because most of the changes came early in his term, the change seemed more abrupt than it actually was. A New Yorker defended the Democrats' patronage policy in these words: "If they are defeated, they expect to retire from office. If they are successful, they claim, as a matter of right, the advantages of success. They see nothing wrong in the rule that to the victor belongs the spoils of the enemy." After this speech, the awarding of public offices to political supporters was called the **spoils system**.

Awarding cabinet positions also involved patronage. Jackson gave cabinet positions to men from different parts of the country. Secretary of State Martin Van Buren represented the North. Vice President Calhoun chose three other southerners. Two positions went to westerners. Because of the conflicts among the official cabinet members, Jackson often sought the opinions of old political friends who held minor government jobs. They met at the White House, often entering the kitchen door to avoid publicity. This unofficial cabinet soon became known as the "kitchen cabinet."

Jackson's strong nationalistic foreign policy pleased all sections of the country. This policy, along with his patronage system, helped to hold the coalition together.

Western Jacksonians wanted a liberal land policy. The ensuing debate led to Daniel Webster's eloquent and dramatic assertion, "It is, sir, the people's Constitution, the people's government; made for the people, made by the people, and answerable to the people." Within the limits of the powers granted by the Constitution, Webster said, the federal government must be the supreme authority; otherwise, the Union would be no more than "a rope of sand." He closed with the famous plea, for "Liberty and Union, now and forever, one and inseparable." Following Webster's speech, Congress returned to the land policy issue. Congress eventually passed a measure permitting **squatters** to buy, for the actual cost of a survey, the land they were living on and were cultivating.

Jackson vetoed a bill for internal improvement within the boundaries of a single state, saying that the states should be responsible for their own improvements. However, he did approve a number of projects that involved two or more states. He also spent a great deal of money for internal improvements in the federal territories, a strategy that regained many western votes lost in the earlier vetoes of projects within states.

The task of removing the Indians to the Louisiana Territory had begun during Jefferson's administration but had proceeded slowly. During Jackson's term, several states decided to take matters into their own hands. Georgia claimed all the Cherokee lands within the state boundaries, even though the Indians held title to the land by federal treaties. The Cherokees had adopted the white man's way of life—cultivating their fields, operating schools, and even publishing a newspaper. Threatened with the loss of lands, the Cherokees appealed to the United States Supreme Court. John Marshall ruled that Georgia had no right to jurisdiction in Cherokee Territory. The Supreme Court had no jurisdiction to enforce its ruling, however. When Jackson refused to use federal troops to protect the Cherokee tribe, the state militia forced the Indians out of Georgia along the "Trail of Tears" to Oklahoma.

When a new tariff was passed, the rates were not substantially lowered. Calhoun began immediately to rally opposition in South Carolina. A special state convention nullified the tariffs of 1828 and 1832. Calhoun resigned the vice presidency and was immediately elected to the Senate by South Carolina. Jackson confidently met the challenge. In a Nullification Proclamation, he stated that he considered the right of a state to nullify a law incompatible with the existence of the Union. He asked Congress to pass a Force Bill empowering him to use the army and navy of the United States against South Carolina if it resisted federal customs officials. No other states joined South Carolina in its resistance, and eventually a compromise was reached with the help of Henry Clay.

The Compromise Tariff of 1833 side-stepped the major issues at stake between the North and the South. However, it did provide temporary relief from the tension aroused by these issues, and it allowed Jackson to restore order within the Democratic Party. It also permitted the president to concentrate on his war against the national bank. Jackson was too shrewd to think that any permanent solution had been reached. He fully expected the "nullifiers in the South...to blow up a storm on the slave question next."

Jackson felt that the national bank had caused the Panic of 1819 and that it enabled eastern businessmen to make money at the expense of southern planters and western farmers. The charter for the bank would not expire until 1836, but proponents of the bank (who were opponents of Jackson) believed that the issue could break Jacksonian power. Therefore, they asked for recharter in 1832. When Jackson vetoed the bank bill, he said that "authority of the Supreme Court must not...be permitted to control the Congress of the Executive when acting in the legislative capacities." The Supreme Court had ruled that the bank was constitutional. Rechartering the bank became the issue for both parties in 1832. Reelection was a triumph for Jackson and the anti-bank forces.

Jackson gradually began to withdraw funds from the national bank and to place them along with incoming funds in chosen state banks, which became known as the administration's "pet banks." Jackson's fight against the bank brought financial troubles during the last years of his administration. Nicholas Biddle, the president of the national bank, was not one to accept defeat. During 1834, he recalled bank loans and refused to make new ones. In 1835 he suddenly reversed his position and lent large sums of money on unusually generous terms. Moreover, the number of state banks more than doubled between 1829 and 1837; and their circulation of bank notes tripled. Both the "pet banks" and other state banks lent money on easy terms. Most of the paper money they issued declined in value; some of it was worthless from the beginning. Biddle's action and the policies of state banks caused a sharp increase in the amount of money in circulation, which led in turn to a rise in prices, or **inflation**.

Distribution of surplus funds in the treasury was still another unsettling factor. By 1835 government revenue from the sale of western land and from tariff duties was sufficient to pay off the national debt. After that time, money accumulated in the treasury faster than the government could spend it. Clay proposed that the surplus money be distributed among the states, hoping they would use it for internal improvement projects. Jackson opposed this plan, but eventually he signed an act providing for the distribution of $28 million among the states.

Worried by the mushrooming inflation, Jackson tried to slow it down. Striking at what he believed was the root of the problem, the president decided to reduce the amount of paper money in circulation and to replace it with specie (coins of gold and silver) which has a stable value. In 1836 he issued the Specie Circular which directed that in the future public lands were to be sold only for specie. Jackson's opponents accused him of high-handed methods in using an executive order which needed no approval from Congress. They hoped this charge would work against an associate of "King Andrew," Martin Van Buren, in the coming election.

The unsettled economy brought new difficulties for Jackson's successor. Van Buren was overwhelmed by the Panic of 1837 and the resulting depression. The trouble stemmed in part from the effects of Jackson's Specie Circular, which had abruptly ended western land speculation and started runs on banks; but the depression which followed and the panic itself were world-wide and probably would have afflicted the United States anyway. British capitalists began calling American loans, halting construction projects throughout the United States, and forcing thousands of laborers out of their jobs.

Rise of the Whigs. The Democrats' inability to cope with the economic troubles of the late 1830s explains the Whigs' rise to power in 1840. However, Whig harmony was destroyed by President William Henry Harrison's unexpected death a month after his inauguration. Harrison was succeeded by his vice president, John Tyler. By the close of the Tyler administration in 1844, both the Whigs and the Democrats had changed their views. The Democrats were more sympathetic toward the South and were taking a much friendlier view of states' rights and strict construction than they had in Jackson's time. The Whigs were inclined toward the North. They were suspicious of the doctrine of states' rights and strongly attached to Webster's concept of an "inseparable" Union. Both parties, however, still drew votes from all sections of the country, and both were openly bidding for the support of the West.

National Archives

William Henry Harrison

Choose one.

3.39   Jackson's Indian policy included _____
   a. a refusal to use federal troops to protect the Cherokee tribe.
   b. an appeal to the Supreme Court for authority to move the Cherokees from Georgia.
   c. support of the northeastern humanitarians who urged a just Indian policy.
   d. the signing of treaties with tribes whereby the Indians received better lands than they gave up.

3.40   Jackson's political strength rested on the solid support of the _____ .
   a. people
   b. politicians
   c. wealthy
   d. well-known

3.41   New opportunities for the American people educationally, economically, and politically were opened by _____ .
   a. Jefferson
   b. Adams
   c. Jackson
   d. Van Buren

3.42   Jacksonian democracy had its roots in the _____
   a. administration of a "wise and frugal government."
   b. Jeffersonian belief in the worth of the individual.
   c. support by the rich and "well-born."
   d. worth of the individual and basic teaching of God's Word.

3.43   Awarding of cabinet positions by Jackson involved _____ .
   a. experience
   b. aptitude
   c. patronage
   d. probation

3.44   What did Jackson's unofficial cabinet became known as? _____
        a. "the parlor cabinet"
        b. "the kitchen cabinet"
        c. "the executive cabinet"
        d. "the White House cabinet"

Fill in the blanks.

3.45   The Northeast favored restrictions on the sale of public lands because
        manpower was being lost to the _____ .

3.46   Daniel Webster was _____ sectionalism.

Adult Check _____
              Initial   Date

· ·
▬ ▬

Before you take this last Self Test, you may want to do one or more of these self checks.

1. ____ Read the objectives. Determine if you can do them.
2. ____ Restudy the material related to any objectives that you cannot do.
3. ____ Use the SQ3R study procedure to review the material:
        a. Scan the sections.
        b. Question yourself again (review the questions you wrote initially).
        c. Read to answer your questions.
        d. Recite the answers to yourself.
        e. Review areas you didn't understand.
4. ____ Review all activities and Self Tests, writing a correct answer for each
        wrong answer.

SELF TEST 3

Choose the best answer(s) (each answer, 2 points).

3.01   As Chief Justice of the United States Supreme Court, John Marshall _____
    a. was a strong Federalist and nationalist.
    b. supported a relatively broad interpretation of federal power.
    c. delivered a series of the most momentous decisions in American judicial history.
    d. all of the above.

3.02   The Panic of 1819 was caused by _____ .
    a. the rapid expansion of American manufacturing
    b. land speculation in the west
    c. postwar competition from British manufacturers
    d. all of the above.

3.03   The political balance between slave and free states as of 1819 was disturbed by _____
    a. Northern abolitionists who succeeded in passing a law to abolish slavery in all the states.
    b. Nat Turner's slave rebellion.
    c. the petition of the territory of Missouri for admission to the Union as a slave state.
    d. all of the above.

3.04   The Missouri Compromise of 1820 provided that _____
    a. Missouri be admitted as a slave state.
    b. Maine be admitted as a free state.
    c. slavery was prohibited in the Louisiana Purchase north of the 36° 30' north latitude line, with the exception of Missouri.
    d. all of the above.

3.05   The striking feature of the Jacksonian era was _____
    a. men of good family rising quickly to positions of great economic and political power.
    b. the disappearance of social classes.
    c. the beginning of American democracy.
    d. an increase in the influence of the common man.

3.06   What did Jackson's unofficial cabinet became known as? _____
    a. "the parlor cabinet"
    b. "the kitchen cabinet"
    c. "the executive cabinet"
    d. "the White House cabinet"

3.07   Jackson's Indian policy included _____
    a. a refusal to use federal troops to protect the Cherokee tribe.
    b. an appeal to the Supreme Court for authority to move the Cherokees from Georgia.
    c. support of the northeastern humanitarians who urged a just Indian policy.
    d. the signing of treaties with tribes whereby the Indians received better lands than they gave.

3.08   Two reasons more settlers moved westward after the War of 1812 were _____ , _____ .
    a. more jobs were available out West
    b. there was plenty of cheap land
    c. Indian hostilities had been crushed for the moment
    d. travel to the West was easy

True/False (each answer, 2 points).

3.09 _____ During the Jacksonian era, more white males gained the right to vote than ever before.

3.010 _____ Through the "spoils system" government positions were filled by trained civil servants regardless of party affiliation.

3.011 _____ The election of 1824 was settled in the House of Representatives, since none of the four candidates had polled a majority in the electoral college.

3.012 _____ Andrew Jackson was the first president who did not come from a well-established American family in comfortable circumstances.

3.013 _____ Jackson was a strong advocate of Calhoun's doctrine of nullification.

3.014 _____ Jackson opposed the national bank because he felt that it allowed eastern business-men to make money at the expense of farmers.

Fill in the blank (each answer, 3 points).

3.015 The policy that European nations should not interfere with America was known as the

_____ .

3.016 The settlers in the West wanted _____ to allow them to ship produce to eastern markets.

3.017 The Erie Canal cut the travel time between Buffalo and Albany from 20 days to _____ days and reduced freight rates by _____ per ton.

Match these men with their accomplishments (each answer, 2 points).

3.018 _____ James Monroe   a. sold the Louisiana Territory to the United States

3.019 _____ Daniel Webster   b. proposed construction of the Erie Canal

3.020 _____ Napoleon   c. opposed the Tariff of 1816

3.021 _____ Andrew Jackson   d. strengthened the influence of the Supreme Court

3.022 _____ DeWitt Clinton   e. wrote the "Star-Spangled Banner"

3.023 _____ Oliver Hazard Perry   f. the secretary of state who supported the Monroe Doctrine

3.024 _____ John C. Calhoun   g. resigned as Jackson's vice president

3.025 _____ Francis Scott Key   h. succeeded James Madison as president

3.026 _____ John Marshall   i. won the Battle of New Orleans

3.027 _____ Martin Van Buren   j. succeeded Andrew Jackson as president

3.028 _____ John Quincy Adams   k. won the Battle of Lake Erie

Before you take the LIFEPAC Test, you may want to do one or more of these self checks.

1. _____ Read the objectives. Determine if you can do them.
2. _____ Restudy the material related to any objectives that you cannot do.
3. _____ Use the SQ3R study procedure to review the material.
4. _____ Review all activities and Self Tests and LIFEPAC Glossary.
5. _____ Restudy areas of weakness indicated by the last Self Test.